HIPPIAS MINOR

—or—

THE ART OF CUNNING

HIPPIAS MINOR

—or—

THE ART OF CUNNING

A new translation of Plato's
most controversial dialogue

Introduction and artwork by
PAUL CHAN
Translation by SARAH RUDEN
Essay by RICHARD FLETCHER

ΔΕΣΤΕ

HIPPIAS MINOR OR THE ART OF CUNNING
Foreword © 2015 Dakis Joannou
Translation and translator's note © 2015 Badlands Unlimited
Introduction and artwork © 2015 Paul Chan
Socrates 420 © 2015 Richard Fletcher

First printing

Co-published by:

Badlands Unlimited
P.O. Box 320310
Brooklyn, NY 11232
Tel: +1 718 788 6668
operator@badlandsunlimited.com
www.badlandsunlimited.com

The DESTE Foundation for
Contemporary Art
Filellinon 11 & Em. Pappa St.
N. Ionia 142 34, Athens
www.deste.gr

Edited by Paul Chan, Richard Fletcher, Karen Marta
Editorial assistance by Micaela Durand, Matthew So, David Torrone
Research by Phoebe Bachman
Copyedited by Charlotte Carter, Miles Champion

Paper book design by Courtney Andujar
Front cover emblem by Paul Chan
E-book design by Ian Cheng

Enhanced e-book with multimedia content available on Apple iBooks,
Amazon Kindle, and other e-readers.
For more information, visit www.badlandsunlimited.com

Paper book distributed in
the Americas by:
ARTBOOK | D.A.P.
155 6th Avenue, 2nd Floor
New York, NY 10013
www.artbook.com

Paper book distributed in
Europe by:
Buchhandlung Walther König
Ehrenstrasse 4
50672 Köln
www.buchhandlung-walther-koenig.de

Printed in the United States of America

ISBN: 978-1-936440-89-4 · E-Book ISBN: 978-1-936440-90-0

CONTENTS

SOCRATES
EUDIKOS
HIPPIAS
ACHILLES
ODYSEUSS
HOMER
MATHEMATICIAN
GEOMETER
ASTRONOMER
RUNNER
WRESTLER
SINGER
ARCHER
DOCTOR
MORALIST
CRIMINAL

LIST OF ILLUSTRATIONS

The illustrations are comprised of preparatory sketches, drawings, and digital renderings of artworks that make up the exhibition *Hippias Minor* by Paul Chan. *Hippias Minor* premiered at the DESTE Foundation's Slaughterhouse project space on the island of Hydra in Greece on June 15, 2015.

FOREWORD

The reader must be as cunning in interpreting a dialogue
as the author has been artful in composing it.
—CHARLES H. KAHN[1]

When I saw Paul Chan at his exhibition at the Schaulager in 2014, he mentioned that he had begun research into one of Plato's most controversial dialogues, which he believes is misunderstood and is in reality a complex argument for the cunning power of art. I was immediately intrigued and thought, where better than the small Saronic island of Hydra—less than fifty miles from Athens and a place that has long been a haven for artists, musicians, and writers—to launch *Hippias Minor or the Art of Cunning*.

The Slaughterhouse project on Hydra began in 2009 in a completely organic way, with the idea of inviting artists who are in the middle of their careers to create a site-specific work. The

Slaughterhouse is a very special place, somewhat isolated on the craggy coast, and certainly a charged one; also, it is probably DESTE's most open-ended program, one in which the artist is totally unconstrained. Each show begins with a conversation and then continues in the spirit of collaboration.

I think of DESTE as uniquely Greek and the Slaughterhouse as a continuation of the ancient traditions of such places as Eleusis, Samothraki, Delphi, and Delos, where people gathered and the oracles spoke and mysteries took place. There was a secret link that tied all these elements together, a philosophical link. This book and exhibition, which includes a symposium on Hydra in the ancient Greek tradition of debate, are in this same spirit: pretexts for a conversation about the meaning of art.

—Dakis Joannou

1. Charles H. Kahn, *Plato and the Socratic Dialogue: The Philosophical Use of a Literary Form* (Cambridge: Cambridge University Press, 1996), 59.

ACKNOWLEDGMENTS

Hippias Minor or the Art of Cunning would not have been possible without the generosity and dedication of Dakis Joannou and everyone at the DESTE Foundation, including Marina Vranopoulou, Regina Alivisatos, Natasha Polymeropoulos, Kleio Silvestrou, Eugenia Stamatopoulou and Eleni Michailidis. At Badlands Unlimited, Ian Cheng, Micaela Durand, Matthew So, Cassie Raihl, and Nickolas Calabrese worked nights and weekends to ensure the book was produced on schedule. We would also like to thank Sarah Ruden for her remarkable translation of *Hippias Minor* and for being a part of this curious book; Courtney Andujar for the book's wonderful design; Phoebe Bachman for providing invaluable research; and David Torrone, Jessica Jackson, and Parker Bruce for assisting in the editorial and production process. Special thanks to Bill Horrigan at the Wexner Center for the Arts, Marlo Poras, Frederic Tuten, Carol Greene, and Greene Naftali Gallery, who all offered insights and other forms of support for what has been realized in these pages. This book would not exist without "The Owl's Legacy," Chris Marker's thirteen-part video series on the historical and philosophical foundations of ancient Greece. Marker was and will remain—in our hearts and minds—the most cunning one of all: the cat *and* the owl. This book is dedicated to his memory.

—*The Editors*

INTRODUCTION

by Paul Chan

Hippias Minor is one of Plato's early dialogues and arguably the most controversial. In it, he portrays Socrates debating Hippias, a prominent sophist. As the dialogue unfolds, Socrates argues that there is no difference between a person who tells the truth and one who lies, that an intentional liar is better than an unintentional one, and that the good man is the one who willingly makes mistakes and does wrong and unjust things.

It is difficult to reconcile this dialogue with Plato's reputation as a philosopher renowned for his pursuit of such ideals as justice and truth. This is the reason *Hippias Minor* is so confounding. It makes claims that plainly contradict what is generally understood to be Plato's philosophical and moral outlook. But what if those claims are puzzling because they have been misunderstood? What if *Hippias Minor* becomes more comprehensible if we broaden the terms of the dialogue, which in turn renders the claims in their full and original complexity? And what if it was revealed that, rather than being a series of paradoxical moral arguments, *Hippias Minor* is actually a provocative theory about the indispensability of aesthetics to an ethical life? What if Socrates wasn't merely championing the act of lying—as the dialogue has traditionally been interpreted—but, rather, advocating for a novel way of thinking about the political potential of the creative act?

Plato was by his own account uninterested in art. He considered it distracting and perhaps even dangerous if left unfettered. The pleasures and insights to be gained from experiencing art are like so many lures that lead away from what he considered the higher good: philosophy. This is why the kind of aesthetics Plato advocated for (on the rare occasions when he did) mirrored how his philosophy acted and felt—pure, changeless, and unwavering.[1] And the art Plato championed was startlingly austere and minimal, but not like the minimalism one would associate with, say, a Donald Judd sculpture. The very appearance of art as something that one could sensuously consider and appreciate was objectionable to Plato. Beauty, for him, was a painting that didn't use paint.

This way of thinking about art is most emphatically reflected in the *Republic*, Plato's later and most expansive work. Poets such as Homer were banned from Callipolis, his utopian city. Songs with

---

1. James I. Porter, *The Origins of Aesthetic Thought in Ancient Greece: Matter, Sensation, and Experience* (New York: Cambridge University Press, 2010), 87.

multiple harmonies were also prohibited, along with any music played by multistringed instruments.[2] All forms of art must be as "unmixed" as possible, which meant that they must be uncontaminated by plurality or change. Plato wanted art to be as pure as he thought his philosophy was.

In early Platonic works such as *Hippias Minor*, this longing for art and philosophy to be as objective and unadorned as the laws of nature was expressed in a negative way. Rather than define what they ought to be, Plato denigrated those who he believed represented what they were not. Here, the target was Hippias of Elis (c. 470–c. 395 BCE), who was a well-known member of the sophistic movement in the fifth century. During this time in Athens, itinerant teachers of the arts and sciences, known as sophists, catered to the growing demand of the Athenian upper class to learn different bodies of knowledge. For large sums of money, sophists taught methods of rhetoric and a variety of philosophical discourses that, among other things, helped those who could afford it reach even higher stations in Greek society. In other words, philosophy was being sold by sophists in ways not unlike the marketing of higher education today: as a tool for social and political advancement.

Hippias was perhaps the first to combine musical and literary analysis, and was attempting to realize a discursive model for understanding language through musical qualities such as pitch and

2. Plato, *Republic* 399d.

rhythm.[3] But very little of this, or any of Hippias's real thinking, is spelled out in the dialogue that bears his name. It was never Plato's intention to give him a fair hearing. Instead, he used Hippias as a stand-in for sophistry in general, so that he could show how Socrates was superior to the entire sophistic movement in his methods of philosophical thinking. This is how Plato wants us to remember him—as the one who, through informal conversation, gave away his philosophy to anyone willing to listen, and emphasized the interdependency between what one knows and who one is. In other words, philosophy was not about knowing this or that, but *being* this way or that way.[4] Socrates's famous proposition that virtue is knowledge reflects his insistence that what is most worth knowing is a particular know-how or practice concerning what it means to carry oneself in the world.

Plato believed Socrates was sentenced to death in 399 BCE by the city of Athens because he was mistakenly viewed as a sophist. This is perhaps why Plato took such pains to distinguish his teacher from the philosophical circle that—in his eyes—contributed to his death. I think it is also reasonable to suggest that this antagonism toward sophists plays a sizable role in how Plato viewed art and aesthetics, since one of the defining characteristics of sophistry is its intimate relationship with the arts.

3. Porter, *Aesthetic Thought*, 214.
4. Pierre Hadot, *What Is Ancient Philosophy?*, trans. Michael Chase (Cambridge, MA: Harvard University Press, 2002), 29.

Among the sophists, Protagoras (c. 490–c. 420 BCE) is considered the oldest and to be broadly representative of sophist thought. He is perhaps best known for his famous dictum that "man is the measure," which succinctly captures the core of Protagoraean philosophy: that the sum of our experiences lies in how things appear to us. For Protagoras, the world is understood solely through our senses, and philosophy consists of what insights can be gained by how it all looks and feels. He believed in a sort of radical empiricism where the essence of a thing is *nothing but* its appearance. Diogenes Laertius reported that Protagoras even held "that the soul is nothing apart from its sensations."[5] Sensorial experience is key to Protagoras's thinking and to sophistry in general.

This accounts for the sophists' fascination with the arts. By engaging with the work of painters, musicians, and poets, they speculated on how artistic compositions came to embody qualities such as beauty, harmony, or pleasure, so that they could harness (and exploit) those same qualities in their philosophical work. They were also materialists, insofar as they accepted that the arts exist in a material reality. A piece of music needs singers and instruments to conjure the sounds that are to be felt and heard; a sculpture comes into being because it is carved from a piece of marble. For the sophists, exemplary sensory experiences such as those afforded by art must be embodied in some kind of material substance if they are

5. Porter, *Aesthetic Thought*, 214.

17

to be grasped at all. So they sought to understand the phenomena that made forms of expression possible.

Plato disdained the sophists for these reasons. He believed material as such was debased and fundamentally deficient as a medium for expressing what was most exemplary about existence, which he called The Good. This undeniably mystical aspect at the core of Platonic thought is coupled with an insistence that only through the rigorous application of a certain way of thinking could The Good be comprehended. And virtues such as beauty were only realized in what he called the Ideas or Forms, which are not embodied in any kind of material substance and so do not exist in actual reality—they literally do not appear and are not apprehended by the senses at all. For Plato, the fact that sophists engaged with the material presence of art and sensuous experience at all made them suspect. He never tired of accusing the sophists of being inferior philosophers, and this is certainly the case in such later works as the *Republic*. But Plato's own philosophy was still developing when he wrote *Hippias Minor*. He could not rely on a robust and mature set of concepts to defeat Hippias; instead, he had to resort to other—more inventive—means.

†

French historian of ancient philosophy Pierre Hadot has noted how the relationship between Socrates and Plato bears a striking resemblance to that of another teacher and his disciple some five hundred years later—Jesus Christ and the apostle Paul.[6] This connection is especially pertinent in *Hippias Minor* because, like Paul, Plato sought to undermine the notion of law and the order that it decrees. In the later section of the dialogue, Socrates makes the case that the excellent man is one who is knowledgeable at what he excels in. But the more he masters a certain field of endeavor, the more he is capable of manipulating that field to suit his interest and will. This, Socrates claims, creates the possibility that the excellent man is the one most able to deceive others, making an explicit connection between understanding something and exploiting it. He goes on to argue that the one who knows law best is also the one capable of being the most criminal, and the one who uses the law most ably, even when it is being *misused*, is the one most worthy of being praised as excellent:

SOCRATES So, now, to commit a crime is to do something poorly, and not to commit one is a fine thing.

HIPPIAS Yes.

SOCRATES So won't the more able and excellent character, whenever it commits a crime, willfully commit that crime, while the worthless character does so against its will?

6. Hadot, *Ancient Philosophy*, 237.

HIPPIAS It appears so.

SOCRATES So isn't the excellent man the one who has an excellent character, while his opposite has a poor character?

HIPPIAS Yes.

SOCRATES Then it's the mark of an excellent man to commit crimes willfully, while his opposite does so against his will, if indeed the excellent man has an excellent character.

HIPPIAS Well, he does have an excellent character, at any rate.

SOCRATES Then the person who goes wrong and does disgraceful and criminal things, if he does exist, can't be anyone other than the excellent person.[7]

Paul takes a similarly ironic and perverse view of law. In *Letters to the Romans*, Paul links law to sin, and suggests that death is felt first by following the law.

What then should we say? That the law is sin? By no means! Yet, if it had not been for the law, I would not

7. Plato, *Hippias Minor* 376a–b (82-83).

have known sin. I would not have known what it is
to covet if the law had not said, "You shall not covet."
But sin, seizing the opportunity in the commandment,
produced in me all kinds of covetousness. Apart from
the law sin lies dead. I was once alive apart from the
law, but when the commandment came, sin revived
and I died.[8]

I don't interpret this as Paul describing a literal death, but, rather,
a psychosomatic dynamic of law, where, in trying to influence our
behavior through regulations and prohibitions, it also agitates and
excites us physically and emotionally. And it is this excitation that
produces a "deadening" within oneself. Law, for Paul, "deadens"
life by making it manic, and disrupts the potential for inner development because the living is too traumatized by its own repetition
compulsion to follow and fulfill the law that lords over it.

Nomos is the Greek word that corresponds to "law," but it
also translates as "custom" or "convention." The constellation of
meanings that nomos represents reflects how the power to establish
and maintain order is understood in the ancient world. And this is
what the writings of Plato and Paul were working to subvert, using
whatever literary and philosophical means were at their disposal.
They were both working against the law of some order. But this

8. Romans 7:7 (English Standard Version).

is not to say that what was being subverted was merely philosophical or literary. In the case of Paul, he had a very particular
and historical kind of law in mind that he sought to upend. That
law was Roman rule.

Likewise, Plato's target was the sophists, who represented a
kind of intellectual and aesthetic influence that he believed led to
the wrong kind of rule in Athens. So he ridiculed the authority the
sophists claimed and the *nomos* they represented:

> SOCRATES Come on now, Hippias, go right at it and
> scrutinize how this applies to all the fields of knowledge
> one by one: Is there anywhere this works differently?
> At any rate, in the greatest number of the arts you're the
> most intelligent among all humankind, as I once heard
> you boasting, relating in detail the plentiful and enviable
> intelligence you possess, in the public square, next to
> the bankers' tables. You said that one time you arrived at
> Olympia with nothing on you but things you had made
> yourself. First the ring—you started there—that you were
> wearing you said was your own work, since you know
> how to carve rings; and another, a signet ring, was your
> work too, plus an oil scraper and an oil bottle—which you
> yourself had wrought! And then there were the sandals you
> had on, which you said you had cobbled on your own, and
> the cloak and short tunic you said you'd woven on a loom!

And what everybody thought was the most outlandish, and the exhibit of the greatest intelligence, was when you said that the belt you wore around that short tunic was like the Persian ones that extravagant people wear, but that you'd twined it together with your own hands.[9]

Throughout the dialogue Socrates questions the veracity of Hippias's claims as if he was exposing the lies of a con artist, and conflates Hippias's inferior intellect with his talent as an artisan, as though they went hand in hand. But what is less remarked upon is how cunning Socrates is in outwitting Hippias, and the degree to which he is willing to use crafty, even outlandish arguments to make his points. Socrates here is no paragon of virtue but, rather, the shrewd and seasoned philosopher who demonstrates how cunning he must be in order to unmask the hollow authority of an inferior form of thinking.

The dialogue in fact begins with the notion of cunning. Hippias had just given a presentation where he claimed Homer made Achilles the most excellent man among those who had arrived at Troy, with Nestor the most intelligent, and Odysseus the most cunning. Hippias then declares that Achilles is better than Odysseus. Eudicus, who had heard Hippias speak, goads Socrates to praise Hippias for his performance. But instead, Socrates begins

9. *Hippias Minor* 368b–c (61).

to question Hippias about why he believes Achilles is superior to Odysseus, and what he means in using the word *cunning*.

Hippias explains that Achilles is the better man because he tells the truth and speaks plainly, whereas Odysseus is deceitful and therefore not excellent. Socrates hones in on this and questions him further, leading him to conclude that the excellent man cannot also be cunning, and vice versa. Hippias goes on to boast how confident he is about what he knows as true. If law is the language of authority, then certainty is its style.

Socrates chaffs at what Hippias presents and proceeds to attack him like a lawyer conducting a cross-examination, dismantling the notion that someone who is cunning cannot also be excellent. At the end of this first series of arguments Socrates corners Hippias with his reasoning and forces him to admit that the excellent man is the one who is *most* capable of cunning—exactly the opposite of what Hippias initially claimed.

SOCRATES Who then turns out to be deceitful concerning calculation, Hippias? The excellent person, or someone else? The same person in fact is able; and this person is also truthful.

HIPPIAS It looks that way.

SOCRATES Do you see, then, that the same person is deceitful and truthful about these things, and that in no way is the truthful person superior to the deceitful one? There's no doubt that it's the same person, and we're not talking about opposites, as you thought just now.[10]

The Greek word Homer uses to describe Odysseus is *polutropos*, which is how Hippias describes Odysseus as well. And like *nomos*, *polutropos* holds a range of meanings; it can describe deceitfulness but it also means "versatile," "adaptable," "ingenious," "crafty," and "never at a loss." In a recent translation of the *Odyssey*, poet and writer Stephen Mitchell expresses these qualities by translating *polutropos* as "cunning."[11]

How is Odysseus cunning? Homer portrays him as a master storyteller and legendary cheat; he is renowned for devising stratagems and ways of cheating gods and men; he tells grand lies and tall tales; his cunning is, in short, his creative instinct. But it is also bound up with his use of reason, or how he is able to understand and reflect on himself and the situation at hand. He uses reason in order to see what he is able (or not able) to get away with by finding or even inventing choices where none are evident or given.[12] This mindfulness is what distinguishes him from other Homeric heroes, what makes him so prudent and, at the same time, so dangerous.

10. Ibid., 367c–d (58–59).
11. Homer, *The Odyssey*, trans. Stephen Mitchell (New York: Atria Books, 2013).

In other words, the cunning that Odysseus embodies is twofold or dialectical. It is creative, inventive, and resourceful precisely because it is grounded in reason, insofar as reason is actually a creative process in its own right. For what Odysseus characterizes is how understanding what is most real and true about reality enables one to more ably reshape it for one's benefit or pleasure. He survives and endures by the grace of what he knows and what he is capable of imagining and creating. Like an artist. Of course, what he wants most is to make his way back home to Ithaca, not make art. But these notions are not so far apart. Consider that, for the Greeks, the idea of homecoming is intimately tied to the notion of identity.[13] Being *someone* in the ancient world meant *one* had to take the trouble to get into *some* in the first place. This is what has been called "the fruitfulness of trouble" in Odysseus.[14] The sufferings he endures and the calamities that befall him act like different artistic materials, which he uses to forge his identity and win recognition that confirms the value of his own existence. In the *Odyssey*, the way home is itself a grand and singular form of expression.

12. This perspective on Odysseus was developed as part of a series of lectures I delivered at the University of Basel, Switzerland, in February and April 2014. The lectures were entitled, "Odysseus as Artist, Parts I and II."

13. G. E. Dimock, Jr., "The Name of Odysseus," *The Hudson Review* 9 (Spring 1956), 67.

14. Ibid., 69.

† †

A work is not merely a simple reflection of the person who made it. What an artist, poet, or philosopher creates gains import precisely when it stands on its own, without the one who made it standing in the way—or so it has been said. But on the other hand, I think that when a work holds any interest at all for us, it is in part because we discern in what is being expressed traces of the *kind* of person who made it. These traces embedded in the work illuminate how a way of living has enlivened (or deadened) what was made or written. This is similar to the way in which the "grain" of a person's voice embodies the one speaking or singing. The grain is the quality of the sound that expresses the particular shape and path air takes as it travels from the lungs, to the larynx, and out of the mouth. It is, in essence, the "body" in the sound.

Likewise, I am always curious about the body in the work. Marcel Duchamp expressed something similar once when he quipped that what interested him most about Andy Warhol's soup can paintings wasn't the paintings themselves but the mind that thought it would be worth the time and energy to paint them in the first place. That is how I think about the Plato who wrote *Hippias Minor*. What *Hippias Minor* claims sounds so contrary to the way Plato is remembered that it is hard to imagine the same person wrote the *Republic*. Is this Plato?

I think it is *yes* insofar as it is also *no*. The provenance of the work is not in dispute. But clearly it appeared before his understanding of art evolved (or devolved, depending on which side of the fence one is on) to the point where he believed that the most exemplary artistic forms are ones that are not expressed at all; before he viewed aesthetics as merely the study of all the vain and dishonest ways in which artists and poets dress up their ideas in order to reach bigger audiences and achieve greater ambitions; before he found that expressions considered creative could be potentially harmful, even dangerous.

It was Plato before Plato, so to speak. After Socrates martyred himself and became a symbol of moral courage, Plato sought to remember his beloved teacher through what is generally considered his early dialogues. And if *Hippias Minor* is any indication, it was during this period in Plato's life when his philosophy was less stark and more accommodating to how art could contribute to a meaningful existence. And perhaps this is the case because art informed Plato's world. He was an aspiring young philosopher who wrote like a poet, trying to come to terms with the life and death of his teacher, who happened to be the son of a sculptor and who, in his own early life, earned a living as a stone carver and who philosophized like no other—in the spirit of irony, playfulness, inventiveness, and, above all, cunning. In other words, he philosophized like an artist.

It is not hard to imagine that Hippias's arrogant and shortsighted view of Odysseus is what prompted Socrates to launch his provocative defense. For Socrates, excellence does not come from simply being frank and noble but by practicing the very Socratic virtue of understanding oneself and, by implication, one's place in the world. And Odysseus manifests in exemplary fashion how powerful this understanding can be. But what is remarkable is that, in *Hippias*, Socrates uses this power to such cunning ends. He was willing to say whatever it took to discredit his interlocutor, even to lie outright.[15] He was in it to win it.

Hippias Minor resembles an *agon*, which, in Greek, means a contest or debate between two characters. The term is typically used to describe a kind of scene in ancient Greek theater in the fifth century BCE, not only in Tragedy but also in so-called Old Comedy. It is a bit of a stretch to align the dialogue with this kind of work, but not too much of one. *Hippias* is funny in its own perverse way. It is certainly ridiculous, like the plays of Aristophanes, who was one of the Old Comedians. It unfolds like a comedy of errors—or better yet, a comedy of reason.

It is also, it seems to me, about an artistic rivalry. As an artist, I can't help but see the debate between Hippias and Socrates as a contest between two different schools of thinking about art. In one corner there is Hippias, who represents the School of Excellence.

15. For a fascinating analysis of how Socrates intentionally misquotes Homer, see Laurence Lampert, "Socrates' Defense of Polytropic Odysseus: Lying and Wrong-doing in Plato's *Lesser Hippias*," in *The Review of Politics* 64, no. 2 (2002), 231–59.

He believes art is best when it serves authority and the kind of law and order it brings (*nomos*). In the other corner there is Socrates, who is head of the School of Cunning. He believes art holds an altogether different purpose, one that serves nobody (*outis*) and reaches its full creative potential only when it is empowered by wild reason (*polutropos*).

There is no real contest, of course. Plato made sure of that. But in the process of intellectually dismantling what he believed Hippias stood for, Plato ends up doing something very unlike him, or who he became, at least. He champions an artistic idea that is as politically subversive as it is surprising, which Socrates performed to full effect: that what is most excellent about the creative act is its power to make a mockery out of any authority, even the authority within oneself.

1. TWO PETALS
2. TWO LEGS
3. LEANING KANT
4. ANTIGONE
5. WENDERS
6. PRAYER

7. CHROUS
8. TRASH

9. KANT REDUX
10. COLUMN
11. TRIO

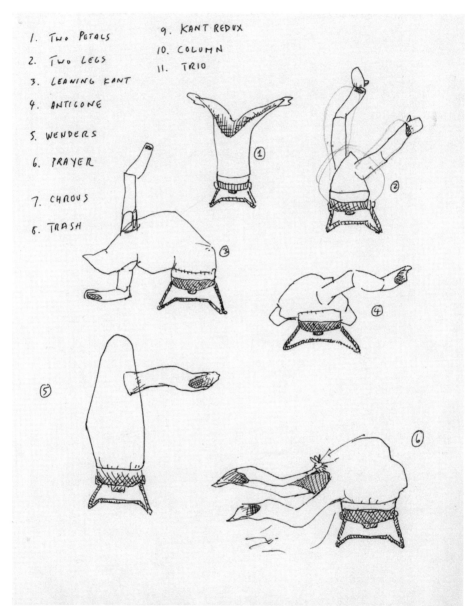

616-295-3737

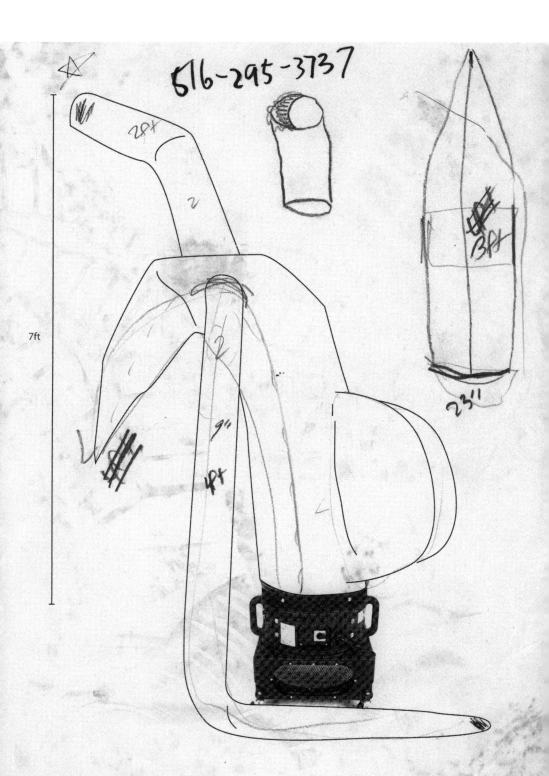

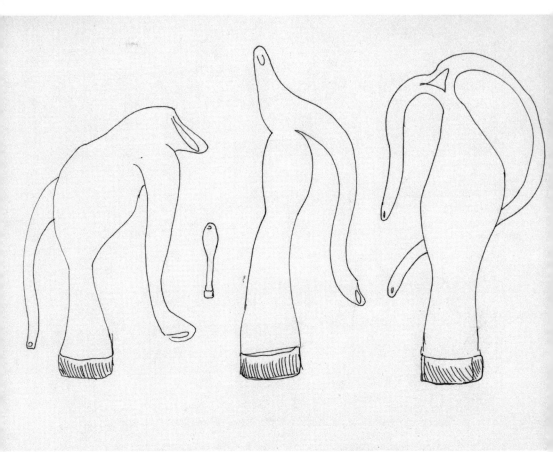

TRANSLATOR'S NOTE

by Sarah Ruden

I need first to confess that I didn't come to this project as a fan of Plato—quite the opposite. He seemed to me, compared to the poets, novelists, and scriptural authors of the ancient world with whom I've been mainly occupied during thirty years as a translator, to be like Marx or Freud: a sweeping theorist whose views, though perhaps appealing to the imagination and the intuition, do not stand up to logic or experience.

But translating this dialogue has given me a chance to see Plato more clearly as a literary artist, and through that to appreciate his ideas more. As always in ancient works, there is a tight cohesion between style and content. To come to grips with an author's diction is to gain a better understanding of mood and theme—and sometimes even of plot or argument—than a stylistic analysis of a modern book would bring.

Ancient literature, being typically performed in public—or, as in the case of Plato, being largely an offshoot of public performance—is hard to separate from the author's personality and the immediate circumstances of composition; and the most important of these circumstances is language: not an incredibly broad and flexible globalized language like modern English, but a proud and narrow means by which people experienced both their inherited belief systems and an absorbing set of daily and festival activities. As it happens, a close look at what Plato's words mean in context—the context not only on the page, but outside it—shows him luxuriating in a homey, rather smug (if competitive) world of Hellenic wealth and culture even as the abstractions he explores invite him to look beyond that world.

In the brief dialogue *Hippias Minor*, Plato uses the traditional vocabulary of performance to ask what can properly be considered performance. Is it—as would probably have been the unreflecting common view—pretty much everything, so that a person's treatment of others comes under the same heading as his athletic or musical or mathematical ability, rendering him almost comprehensively the prisoner of his talent and skill? He could then, absurdly, be blamed more for his crimes because, without the self-control of an expert, he commits them unwillingly. This dead end of the dialogue isn't really a dead end but instead looks forward to the collectivist and totalitarian arguments of *Republic*. Why not just let the state take control of human difference, since individuals cannot help who they are?

But to explain how I came to see this in the dialogue requires some backtracking through the translation methods I've developed over the years, and the ways I've applied them to this particular task. They are, in fact, fairly simple, being based on a single circumstance: the literary vocabulary of Latin, Greek, and Hebrew is relatively tiny, and the important words around which discourse turns are multipurpose, previously rather vague ones. Classical authors manipulated them in various directions rather than quickly nailing them down in any one place. These meanings in the process of development were loaded with irony, ambiguity, and drama in many of their uses, requiring an alert, critical spectatorship of the words as actors. At length, of course, there emerge fixed, specialized vocabularies, like the Greek philosophical vocabulary, that can be shown in glossaries or specialized dictionaries. Essential as such tools are—it is impossible to imagine addressing a language, a literature, or a cultural history without them—they do not get translators off the hook. The intrigue and adventure of vocabulary *formation* have to be staged somehow.

The fifth-century Greek word *sophos*, for example, could have meanings as various as "smart-aleck" and "talented." A translator can range among these, or adopt a single, potentially far-reaching rendering like "intelligent" (my own choice for *Hippias Minor*). But to translate *sophos* consistently as "wise" is to read backwards, hurling into the past the results of many centuries of intellectual development, at the end of which there was a fixed (and fusty, to the point of comedy) concept of a special intelligence that is moral, venerable, and transcendent—wisdom. We can, however, see fascinating moments in that development, particularly in Plato the dramaturge. He may even be playing at reading backwards himself in his depiction of the *sophos* Hippias, who can deliver dazzling, if shallow, speeches the way Netflix delivers films, and can carve rings to boot. But then Plato busies himself with writing forward: How will Socrates proceed to enact the quality of *sophia* in dealing with Hippias?

In translating *Hippias Minor*, I assembled a list of words needing English counterparts that were as neutral as possible while still being malleable, so that readers could follow the words' fates—which comprise the only plausible sense in this otherwise quite baffling dialogue. (Less important words I varied almost at will for the sake of euphony, to fit different contexts, and to avoid monotony; Plato with consistent vocabulary throughout would be very dull and require excessive scholarly glossing.) Here, besides *sophos*, are the essentials:

Kalos: Not "beautiful," an English word closely attached to aesthetics. Plato's *kalos* can be that as well, but also means practically or morally "fine"—my translation throughout. In Socrates's mouth, Plato's "fine" can be either casual or earnest or have a sharp ironic edge.

Agathos, ameinōn, aristos; beltiōn, beltistos: With these words, Plato pulls a fast one invisible to readers of ordinary English translations.

Agathos has "good" (which, when applied to a person, we normally understand as "morally good") as only one of its meanings, which is rare until late in the word's evolution. Ordinarily in Plato's time and before, people favored the meanings "noble" and "brave" and "skillful"; I translate it as "excellent." *Ameinōn* and *aristos*, the comparative and superlative, follow that sense pretty faithfully—"superior" and "most excellent." But *beltiōn* and *beltistos* are another comparative and superlative branching from the same word, both of them less personal and more mundane, more suggestive of ethics—"more fitting" and "most fitting," I translate, marking clearly where Socrates simply changes the terms of the argument and is no longer speaking of qualities inherent in Homeric warriors but of qualities more proper to the Athenian way of life (yet Hippias is not shown calling Socrates on this). The kicker is that both superlatives are commonly used, and used in this dialogue, as polite (and sometimes politely sarcastic) forms of address. The difference is not arbitrary, and both should not be translated as "Sir" or "My dear friend."

Polutropos: "Cunning," not "of many twists and turns" or "of many wiles" or any other colorfully precise term. Plato lets the word spread, in the reader's imagination, minimally across Odysseus's adventures, and the hero is not only good at intrigue and ambush but good at boat-building and storytelling and other practical arts. We do in English sometimes speak of cuteness or fine workmanship as "cunning." (The Homeric epithet quoted in the dialogue to describe Odysseus is the related *polumēchanos*, which I've translated as "of the cunning devices.")

Psuchē: Not "soul"—which would too easily import Plato's own startling innovation along the lines of an "immortal soul"—the *psuchē* was normally the inner life, the mind, the energy, the nature. A true all-purpose translation is impossible, so I'm driven to look at the specific needs of *Hippias Minor* and don't feel I can do better than "character." Under discussion is not only the performance of a citizen in competition but the serviceability of a horse or a slave, how reliable it is for its owner. Character is our go-to word for the inherent capability (*dunatos*, "able," is endlessly repeated in the dialogue) of a being to perform as needed and expected.

Ergazomai: Not "act" or "work" but "perform." Socrates's question whether "to do is to perform" is not a strange leap, but is based on a ready cultural assumption, to which Plato makes Hippias readily accede: practically anything important is done in public, and is judged (hence I translate *aischros* as "disgraceful" and not "shameful," which for us can describe purely private events and feelings). The dialogue is about the *judgment*, from outside, of persons, things, and actions.

Dikē, dikos, adikia, adikos: No, no, no! Not "justice," "just," "injustice," and "unjust"! In English those words are normally either fairly abstract or connote qualities of powerful entities such as rulers and governments. Here, Plato is instead discussing—explicitly in places, even if among many possibilities for meanings of the words—a person's "lawfulness" or "criminality," his functions within a civilized state. Is this a performance like others, or is it something else? If so, how do we regard it?

HIPPIAS MINOR

—OR—

The Art of Cunning

EUDICUS But you, Socrates—how about it? Why aren't you saying anything? Hippias has given such a great presentation, and you won't join in praising anything that's been said—and you won't put him to the test if something doesn't seem fine to you? A special reason for you to speak up is that it's actually just us on our own here, the people most entitled to claim a share in the pursuit of ideas.

SOCRATES Well, in fact, Eudicus, there are some things Hippias was saying just now concerning Homer that I'd enjoy asking him about. It just so happens that your father, Apemantus, used to say that Homer's *Iliad* is a finer poem than the *Odyssey*, and that it's finer inasmuch as Achilles is *superior* to Odysseus— given that one of the two compositions concerns Odysseus, and the other, Achilles. So on this issue I'd enjoy questioning Hippias thoroughly, if he's willing, as to his opinion about these two men.

Which one does he say is superior? He has, you see, presented for our benefit all *sorts* of other things, about Homer as well as other poets.

EUDICUS   Naturally! I'm certain Hippias won't hold out but will answer anything you ask him. Isn't that so, Hippias? If Socrates asks you something, will you answer? What else would you do?

HIPPIAS   Quite right, Eudicus! It would be terrible if I didn't answer. I go to Olympia to the festival of all the Greek states during the Olympic games; every time, I go back there from my home in Elis, and I enter the sanctuary and make myself available to give any speech anyone wants—out of the ones I've prepared to present—and I answer any question anyone wants to ask me. It would be terrible for me to run away now from Socrates's questioning.

SOCRATES   This is a blessed fate you've found, Hippias, if at each Olympiad you're so sanguine, when you arrive at the sanctuary, about the way your character serves your intelligence. I would marvel if any athlete comes to that place as fearless and full of conviction about his means of contending—the body, that is—as you are about your thinking.

HIPPIAS It stands to reason, Socrates, that this is what I've found, since from the time I started to contend at the Olympics, I never encountered anyone with more mastery than I had.

SOCRATES I guess, Hippias, that you're saying this renown of yours for intelligence is a fine offering to the city and to your parents too. Fair enough, but what have you got to say to us about Achilles and Odysseus? Which one is superior, and what do you say makes him superior? When a lot of us were indoors there, you know, and you were making your presentation, I lost track of what you were saying. I shrank from asking question after question, because there was a big crowd in there and I didn't want to get in the way of your presentation with my queries. But now, because there are fewer of us, and Eudicus here urges me to ask, do say, and instruct us clearly: What did you mean about those two men? How were you distinguishing between them?

HIPPIAS Just leave it to me, Socrates: I want to go through, in detail, even more clearly than I did then, what I mean both about them and about other men. I say that Homer made Achilles the most excellent man among those who had arrived at Troy, Nestor the most intelligent, and Odysseus the most cunning.

SOCRATES Dear, oh dear, Hippias! You could do me a huge favor by not making fun of me, if I'm a slow learner of what you say and keep asking questions all the time. Instead, try to answer me gently and patiently.

HIPPIAS It would be disgraceful for me—given that I school other people in these very things and think myself worth being paid because of what I teach—if I didn't show sympathy and answer your queries gently.

SOCRATES That's an altogether fine thing to say! I myself, you see, when you said that Homer had shown Achilles to be the most excellent—I seemed to understand what you meant, and also when you said that Nestor was the most intelligent. But when you said about Odysseus that the poet, in his poem, had made him the most cunning—as to this, to be truthful with you, I absolutely don't know what it is you mean. So tell me, and give me a chance to learn something more from what you say. Hasn't Achilles been shown by Homer to be cunning?

HIPPIAS Hardly, Socrates, but instead he's the most frank and truthful, since in the part called "The Prayers," when Homer shows them arguing with each other, he has Achilles saying to Odysseus,

> Son of Laertes, descended from Zeus, Odysseus of the cunning devices,
> I must give my account—I don't care what you say—

Of how I mean to carry this out, and how I think it will be

accomplished.

I am the enemy, implacable as hell's gates,

Of the man who hides one thing in his heart and says another.

But I will speak, and it will be accomplished.

In these lines he shows the personality of either man, Achilles being truthful and frank, while Odysseus is cunning and deceptive: he shows this in the lines he makes Achilles speak to Odysseus.

SOCRATES So already, Hippias, I have a good chance of learning what you mean. You mean the cunning man is deceptive—it appears so, at any rate.

HIPPIAS Exactly, Socrates. That's how Homer has depicted Odysseus everywhere in the *Iliad* and the *Odyssey*.

SOCRATES Then Homer, it seems, thought that the one was a truthful man and the other a deceptive one—the same man isn't both.

HIPPIAS Well, yes, why wouldn't that be the case, Socrates?

SOCRATES Do you yourself think so too, Hippias?

HIPPIAS Nothing's more certain than that I do. It would in fact be terrible if I didn't.

SOCRATES Well then, we can just let Homer alone, since at any rate it's impossible to interrogate him about what on earth was on his mind when he wrote those lines. You, however, since you appear to be taking on the responsibility here, and you agree with Homer on these exact things you claim he means, answer jointly on behalf of Homer and yourself as well.

HIPPIAS We can proceed that way. Ask whatever you want to, but keep it short.

SOCRATES Do you mean that deceptive people are such that, like the sick, they're unable to do something, or that they're able to do something?

HIPPIAS I mean, of course, that they're able—most definitely able, particularly when they con people.

SOCRATES Then, as it appears, they're able, and they're cunning—according to your version of it. Is that the case?

HIPPIAS Yes.

SOCRATES   But are they cunning and tricky from simplemind-edness and empty-headedness or from cynicism and a sort of shrewdness?

HIPPIAS   From cynicism, most certainly, and shrewdness.

SOCRATES   Then they're shrewd, it seems.

HIPPIAS   Yes, by Zeus—excessively so, in fact.

SOCRATES   Being shrewd, do they not understand what they're doing, or do they understand?

HIPPIAS   They absolutely understand. That's the reason they do wrong.

SOCRATES   Then understanding these things they understand, are they inept or intelligent?

HIPPIAS   Intelligent, certainly—if only in their trickery.

SOCRATES   Hold on. Let's recall what it is you're claiming. You say that people who deceive are able and shrewd and under-standing and intelligent for the purpose of the things about which they're deceptive.

HIPPIAS That's just what I say.

SOCRATES And the truthful and the deceptive are different classes of people, diametrically opposed to each other?

HIPPIAS This is what I claim.

SOCRATES All right, then: among able and intelligent people, as it appears, some are deceptive, according to your version of it.

HIPPIAS Exactly.

SOCRATES But when you claim that the deceptive are able and intelligent regarding these very things, do you mean that they're able to deceive if they wish to, or that they have no ability as to the things in which they actually deceive?

HIPPIAS I do say that they have the ability.

SOCRATES To sum up what's been said, then, the deceptive are the intelligent and those able to deceive.

HIPPIAS Yes.

SOCRATES Therefore a man unable to deceive, and inept, would not be deceptive.

HIPPIAS That's the way it is.

SOCRATES The able one, then, is every person who can do what he wants at the time he wants to do it. I mean, of course, that he's not prevented by sickness or anything else of that sort. Instead, he's like you: able to write my name whenever you want— to give an example. Or do you not call someone able, when that's the case with him?

HIPPIAS Yes, I do.

SOCRATES So come on, tell me, Hippias, are you not actually an expert in arithmetic, the art of calculation?

HIPPIAS Above all I certainly am, Socrates.

SOCRATES Surely, then, if someone asked you for the sum of three times seven hundred, granted you were willing, you would be the fastest and the most certain in telling the truth about this.

HIPPIAS There's no doubt whatsoever.

SOCRATES That's because you're the most able and the most intelligent in these matters.

HIPPIAS Yes.

SOCRATES But which is it? Are you merely the most intelligent and the most able, or are you also the most excellent in these things in which you are most able and most intelligent, things having to do with calculation?

HIPPIAS Also the most excellent, Socrates, to be sure.

SOCRATES Therefore you would be the most able in making a true pronouncement concerning these things. Is that so?

HIPPIAS I think so, at any rate.

SOCRATES But what about deceitful statements concerning these same things? Though it's just me, do as you did before and answer graciously and loftily, Hippias. Say someone asks you for the sum of three times seven hundred. Would you be the person most certain to act dishonestly and to speak deceitfully about these things, and would you do so consistently—granted, of course, that you wanted to be deceitful and never answer truthfully? Or would a man who is inept about arithmetic be able to deceive more certainly than you could, if he wanted to? Or would the inept man who wished to deceive often speak the truth unwillingly, as it turns out, through his ignorance, but you, as an intelligent man, can always be deceitful in the same way, if you want to?

HIPPIAS Yes, that's the way it is, as you yourself hold.

SOCRATES Then the deceitful person would be deceitful about other things, but not about numbers? He wouldn't be deceitful about numerical matters?

HIPPIAS Yes, he *is*, by Zeus: he's deceitful about numbers too.

SOCRATES Then we can hold this as well, Hippias, that concerning calculation and numbers, a given person is deceitful?

HIPPIAS Yes.

SOCRATES Then who would this person be? Isn't it established that, if he's going to be deceitful, he must be *able* to be deceitful—as you agreed just now? As for the one who's unable to be deceitful, if you recall, it was stated repeatedly by you that he would never be deceitful.

HIPPIAS Um, I remember that it was stated thus.

SOCRATES And didn't you appear just now to be the ablest person to deceive concerning arithmetic?

HIPPIAS Yes, I guess that was stated as well.

SOCRATES But aren't you also most able to state the truth about arithmetic?

HIPPIAS Absolutely.

SOCRATES So isn't the same person most able to deceive *and* tell the truth about arithmetic? This man is the excellent one concerning these things—he's skilled in calculating.

HIPPIAS Yes.

SOCRATES Who then turns out to be deceitful concerning calculation, Hippias? The excellent person, or someone else? The same person in fact is able; and this person is also truthful.

HIPPIAS It looks that way.

SOCRATES Do you see, then, that the same person is deceitful and truthful about these things, and that in no way is the truthful person superior to the deceitful one? There's no doubt that it's the same person, and we're not talking about opposites, as *you* thought just now.

HIPPIAS It *doesn't* appear so—in this case, at any rate.

SOCRATES Do you want us to scrutinize other cases?

HIPPIAS If that's what *you* want.

SOCRATES Aren't you also an expert in geometry?

HIPPIAS I am indeed.

SOCRATES Well, then? Isn't the situation in geometry the same? The same person is most able to deceive and to tell the truth about geometric figures—the one who's skilled in geometry.

HIPPIAS Yes.

SOCRATES In these things is someone else excellent, or is it this person?

HIPPIAS Nobody else.

SOCRATES   Then isn't the excellent and intelligent man who's skilled in geometry most able in either direction? And if any person is deceptive about geometric figures, this would be him, the excellent one? This is in fact the able one. But the poor one would be unable to be deceitful: the result being that the one without the ability to be deceitful would not emerge as deceitful—as was agreed.

HIPPIAS   That's the situation.

SOCRATES   Moving along, let's scrutinize a third person, the astronomer. Now this is a field in which I think you're even more knowledgeable than in those discussed before—is that so, Hippias?

HIPPIAS   Sure.

SOCRATES   Doesn't this very same situation prevail in astronomy?

HIPPIAS   I guess so, Socrates.

SOCRATES   Then in astronomy as well, if we have someone who's deceptive, the excellent astronomer will be deceptive, as the one who's able to deceive; it's not the one who's unable: he's inept!

HIPPIAS   That's how it appears.

SOCRATES   Therefore the same man, in astronomy also, will be both truthful and deceptive.

HIPPIAS   So it seems.

SOCRATES   Come on now, Hippias, go right at it and scrutinize how this applies to all the fields of knowledge one by one: Is there anywhere this works differently? At any rate, in the greatest number of the arts you're the most intelligent among all humankind, as I once heard you boasting, relating in detail the plentiful and enviable intelligence you possess, in the public square, next to the bankers' tables. You said that one time you arrived at Olympia with nothing on you but things you had made yourself. First the ring—you started there—that you were wearing you said was your own work, since you know how to carve rings; and another, a signet ring, was your work too, plus an oil scraper and an oil bottle—which you yourself had wrought! And then there were the sandals you had on, which you said you had cobbled on your own, and the cloak and short tunic you said you'd woven on a loom! And what everybody thought was the most outlandish, and the exhibit of the greatest intelligence, was when you said that the belt you wore around that short tunic was like the Persian ones that extravagant people wear, but that you'd twined it together with your own hands.

Besides these things, you said you had come with poems, both epics and tragedies as well as dithyrambs, and a number of prose compositions of all sorts. And about the arts of which I was speaking just now, you had arrived, according to yourself, with knowledge superior to that of other people; and also about musical beats and harmonies and correct grammar, and ever so many other things I believe I can call to mind. Oh, but it looks as if I forgot your system for memorization, in which you think yourself most illustrious. And I think I've forgotten all manner of other things. But what I'm in fact stating is this: you must actually look at your own arts—and you've got enough of them—and at those of other people and tell me, based on what you and I have agreed between ourselves, whether you can find anywhere an instance where there is a truthful person on the one hand and a deceitful one on the other—where they're separate and not the same person. Look for this in whatever use of intelligence you want to—or in whatever cynical behavior, or whatever you're pleased to call it: in any event you won't find it, my friend, because it doesn't exist. If it does, then tell me about it!

HIPPIAS But I can't, Socrates; not right now, at any rate.

SOCRATES And you're not going to be able to, I think. But if I'm speaking the truth, call to mind what results from our discussion, Hippias.

HIPPIAS   I don't quite understand what you're saying, Socrates.

SOCRATES   Well, perhaps you're not using your system of memorization—it's clear that you don't think you need to—but let me remind you: you know that you said that Achilles was truthful, whereas Odysseus was deceitful and cunning.

HIPPIAS   Yes.

SOCRATES   Now then, do you perceive that the same person has been plainly shown as both deceitful and truthful, so that if Odysseus was deceitful, he also turns out to be truthful, and if Achilles is truthful, he's also deceitful, and that the two men aren't different from each other, and aren't opposites, but are similar.

HIPPIAS   Socrates, you're one to always be twining together some argument or other like this. You're always cutting off whatever part of the argument is the hardest to grasp, and you grab onto it and attach yourself to trivia. You contend in such a way that you don't address the general topic being discussed. So now then, if you like, I'll put on display for you, with many proofs, a quite strong enough argument that Homer depicted Achilles as superior to Odysseus, and not deceptive, whereas he depicted Odysseus as practicing all kinds of deceptions, and inferior to Achilles. If you like, you in your turn can set your argument beside mine and measure the difference, as to the other man being superior. And these men here will see for themselves which of us two proves the superior speaker.

SOCRATES Hippias, I'm emphatically not disputing that you're more intelligent than I am. But it's my constant habit, whenever anybody states anything, to apply my mind, especially whenever the speaker seems to me to be intelligent. And since I'm eager to learn what he means, I question him searchingly and backtrack in my ponderings and see whether what's been said is consistent, so that I *can* learn. But if the speaker seems to me to be useless, I don't ask those persistent questions, and I don't care what he says. And you'll know by this which people I consider to be intelligent. You'll find me, in fact, relentless about what such a man says, questioning him in order to learn something that will be helpful to me. At present, for example, I noticed something, while you were speaking. Just now you cited verses to demonstrate that Achilles was speaking to Odysseus as if the latter were a charlatan. That seemed to me outlandish—if you're speaking the truth—because Odysseus nowhere is plainly deceptive, though he's cunning, whereas Achilles is plainly a cunning person according to your own argument. He *does* deceive, at any rate. He pronounces these lines, which you did recite just now:

> I am the enemy, implacable as hell's gates,
> Of the man who hides one thing in his heart and says another.

A little after that he states that he won't be induced by Odysseus or
Agamemnon to change his mind and isn't even going to remain at
Troy at all. No, he says,

> Tomorrow, once I have sacrificed to Zeus and all the other gods,
> Loaded my ships securely, and dragged them down to the sea,
> You will see, if you want to—in case you care about it—
> At the break of dawn, on the fish-filled Hellespont, my ships
> Sailing, and the men in them, eagerly rowing.
> And if the glorious Earth-shaker grants us a good voyage,
> On the third day I'll reach Pthia with its rich loam.

And even before this passage, he says, taunting Agamemnon:

> Now I will go to Pthia. Since it is much more agreeable
> To go home with my crook-beaked ships, I don't think
> I'll stay here dishonored, piling up a rich income for you.

Though he says these things at one time in front of the whole army
and at another to his own comrades, he never at any point in the
story appears to have prepared or undertaken to haul down his
ships with the intention of sailing home. No, instead he shows a
thoroughly aristocratic disregard for telling the truth. For my part,
Hippias, from the very beginning, I questioned you because I was
at a loss as to which of the two men was shown by the poet to be

superior. I assumed that both are most excellent and that it's hard to judge which is superior in deception or the truth or in any other distinction. Both in fact are roughly equal in this respect.

HIPPIAS   But that's not a fair way to look at it, Socrates. In Achilles's deceptions, he doesn't appear to me deceiving deliberately but unwillingly, because of the disaster that befalls the army, which forces him to remain and come to the rescue. But Odysseus's deceptions *are* willing and deliberate.

SOCRATES   Come off it, my priceless Hippias! You're just conning me now. You're playing the part of Odysseus yourself.

HIPPIAS   Absolutely not, Socrates! What on earth do you mean, and why would you say such a thing?

SOCRATES   You say Achilles isn't deliberately deceptive, whereas he was such a cheat, so deliberate a charlatan, as Homer depicted him, that he appears shrewder than Odysseus in effortlessly playing the bragging charlatan with him and not even being suspected of doing so. He's shrewd to the extent that, face to face with him, he has the gall to completely contradict himself—and Odysseus has no idea. At any rate, in no way whatsoever is Odysseus shown, while speaking to him, to perceive that the man is being deceptive.

HIPPIAS   What's this you're telling me, Socrates?

SOCRATES   You don't know that, after telling Odysseus that
he'll sail away as soon as it's dawn, he turns around and tells Ajax
not that, but something else?

HIPPIAS   Where's that?

SOCRATES   It's in these lines; he says,

> I won't take any interest in bloodstained war
> Before the son of brilliant Priam, shining Hector,
> Reaches the Myrmidons' camp and their ships
> As he slaughters the Argives, and their black ships dissolve in his fire.
> But when he's near my lean-to, and my black ship,
> Hector, though eager, will hold off from fighting, I think.

So do you actually think, Hippias, that the son of Thetis and
the man who had been schooled by the superlatively intelligent
Chiron was so forgetful that, whereas a little before he was
berating "charlatans" in the nastiest terms, he could say to
Odysseus that he was sailing away, but to Ajax that he was staying,
without doing it deliberately and counting on Odysseus's being
senile, and on getting the better of him by using this actual contriv-
ance and deception?

HIPPIAS I certainly don't think so, Socrates. Instead, he was prompted by good-heartedness to say something different to Ajax than to Odysseus. But as for Odysseus, he's deliberate both in stating the truth and in deceiving; it's just the same for him.

SOCRATES Then Odysseus is apparently superior to Achilles.

HIPPIAS That's absolutely not the case, Socrates.

SOCRATES What then? Wasn't it made clear just now that those who deceive willingly are more fitting persons that those who do so unwillingly?

HIPPIAS But how can it be, Socrates, that those who willingly commit crimes and are willfully and deliberately treacherous and perform evil acts are more fitting persons than the unwilling? For these there seems to be much forbearance—in cases, that is, where, without being aware of it, someone commits a crime or a deception or does some other evil thing. And the laws are in fact much harsher toward those who willfully perform evil acts and practice deception than toward the unwilling.

SOCRATES You see, Hippias, that I'm telling the truth, that I'm stubborn in interrogations of intelligent people, and I probably have only this single excellence, whereas everything else about me is totally useless. You see, I get tripped up in trying to see what the state of affairs is, and I don't know what's going on. For me, sufficient evidence of this is that, whenever I meet one of you people who are celebrated for your intelligence, people to whose intelligence all the Greeks bear witness, it appears that I know nothing. There's basically no opinion of yours that I share. So then what greater evidence of ineptitude is there than when someone differs from intelligent gentlemen? But I do have one amazing excellence, which redeems me: I see no disgrace in learning—no, I inquire, I ask my questions, and I evince great gratitude toward the person who answers me. There's no one I ever defrauded of gratitude; in fact, I never repudiated having learned something, making out that the thing learned was my own discovery, but instead I pronounce a panegyric on the intelligence of the person who taught me, and I proclaim what I learned from him. But on this particular occasion, I don't agree with what you state; I couldn't disagree more strongly. But I do know that I'm responsible for this, because I am the way I am, which is the reason I make no kind of inflated claim about myself.

Well, Hippias, everything does appear to me to be the opposite of what you state it to be. It is my considered opinion that those who harm people and commit crimes and deceive and trick and go the wrong way willingly—not unwillingly—are more fitting persons than those who do these things unwillingly. However, sometimes

I hold the opposite opinion. I'm at a loss, and it's clearly because of my ignorance. But at this point I'm suffering an episode of brain fever, so to speak, and those who of their own free will go completely wrong in some way in fact seem to me to be more fitting persons than those who do so unwillingly. The blame for my present suffering I place on the arguments set out before, with the result that *at this point* it's plain that those who unwillingly do each of these things are a more worthless sort of people than those who act willingly.

Therefore, do me a favor and don't begrudge putting my character in a better state. It's really a more excellent piece of work for you to relieve my character of this ineptitude than to relieve my body of disease. If you wish to deliver a long speech, however, I warn you that you wouldn't heal me that way, because I couldn't follow you. But if you wish to answer me as you did just now, you'll help me comprehensively, and I don't think it will harm yourself either. And with justice I appeal to you, child of Apemantus, as you induced me to have this exchange with Hippias: so now, if Hippias doesn't want to answer me, ask him on my behalf.

EUDICUS Oh, no, Socrates, I don't think the situation demands, or maybe I should say, that we demand this of Hippias. What he said beforehand wouldn't indicate that: on the contrary, he said that he wouldn't run away from any gentleman's questioning. Isn't that right, Hippias? Isn't that what you stated?

HIPPIAS   I did indeed. But Socrates is always making trouble in the course of discussions, and it's almost as if he's up to no good.

SOCRATES   Oh, nobody fits the bill better than you do, Hippias! I'm not at any rate doing it willingly. If I did, I would be intelligent and terribly clever, according to your argument. But no, I'm doing it unwillingly, so show me forbearance. You say, remember, that if someone is unwillingly up to no good, it's necessary to be forbearing with him.

EUDICUS   By no means, Hippias—don't do differently now. Both for our sake and for the sake of the statements you made before, answer Socrates, whatever he asks.

HIPPIAS   Yes, I'll answer, since it's you asking. Go on then, ask whatever you want to.

SOCRATES   Oh, good, because I'm very keen, Hippias, to make a thorough examination of what was stated just now, concerning *which* of these two classes is superior, the ones who go wrong willingly, or unwillingly. I think, then, that this is the most straightforward way to approach this examination. Answer, now. Do you call a certain kind of runner excellent?

HIPPIAS   I do.

SOCRATES And another kind poor?

HIPPIAS Yes.

SOCRATES So then isn't the one who runs well an excellent runner, and the one who runs poorly a poor one?

HIPPIAS Yes.

SOCRATES In a race, then, and in running, speed is excellent, and slowness is poor?

HIPPIAS How else would it be?

SOCRATES Is the superior runner therefore the one who willingly or unwillingly runs slowly?

HIPPIAS Willingly.

SOCRATES Is it not the case that to run is to do something?

HIPPIAS It's doing something, of course.

SOCRATES But if it's doing something, is it not also performing something?

HIPPIAS Yes.

SOCRATES Then the one who runs poorly puts on this poor and disgraceful performance in the race?

HIPPIAS It's a poor one—how could it not be?

SOCRATES And the one running slowly runs poorly?

HIPPIAS Yes.

SOCRATES So then doesn't an excellent runner willingly put on this poor and disgraceful performance, while the poor runner does so unwillingly?

HIPPIAS It seems so, anyway.

SOCRATES In a race, then, the unwilling one is the poorer performer than the willing one?

HIPPIAS In a race, at least.

SOCRATES What about in wrestling? Is the superior wrestler the one who takes a fall willingly or unwillingly?

HIPPIAS Unwillingly, it appears.

SOCRATES Is a fall or a throw a poorer and more disgraceful act in wrestling?

HIPPIAS A fall.

SOCRATES And in wrestling, then, the one who willingly performs poorly and disgracefully is the more fitting wrestler? Or is it the one who does so unwillingly?

HIPPIAS The first, it appears.

SOCRATES What about in every other kind of physical exercise? Is the fitter person not able to perform in both ways with his body, giving both a strong and a weak performance, and a disgraceful and a fine one? This means that when he gives a poor performance with his body, for the fitter person that physical performance is willing, but for the poorer athlete it's unwilling.

HIPPIAS This seems to be the case as far as strength goes.

SOCRATES But what about gracefulness, Hippias? Is it not characteristic of the fitter body to willingly assume disgraceful and poor positions, while the poorer body does this unwillingly? Or what do you think?

HIPPIAS That's right.

SOCRATES Then gracelessness that's willing is meritorious where physical condition is concerned, while gracelessness that's unwilling is a sign of *poor* physical condition.

HIPPIAS That's clear.

SOCRATES And what is your view about the voice? Which do you say is the more fitting, the voice that sings willingly or unwillingly off-key?

HIPPIAS Willingly.

SOCRATES If unwillingly, it would be a more wretched voice?

HIPPIAS Yes.

SOCRATES Would you choose to have excellent attributes or poor ones?

HIPPIAS Excellent ones.

SOCRATES Would you choose to have feet with which you limped willingly or unwillingly?

HIPPIAS Willingly.

SOCRATES Isn't lameness in the feet a worthless and disgraceful condition?

HIPPIAS Yes.

SOCRATES Well then, isn't bad eyesight a worthless condition?

HIPPIAS Yes.

SOCRATES Then what kind of eyes would you rather have, and which kind would you rather have to deal with, the kind with which a person intentionally or unintentionally sees blurrily and mistakes what he sees?

HIPPIAS The ones with which a person willingly does those things.

SOCRATES Then you consider more fitting, in your own case, a poor physical performance that's willing than one that's unwilling?

HIPPIAS At least where such things are concerned.

SOCRATES And overall, where hearing and smelling and taste and the other senses are concerned, doesn't a single principle hold, namely that if they perform badly against a person's will they're not worth having, because they're in a poor state, but that if the person is willing, they *are* worth having, because they're excellent.

HIPPIAS That *is* what I think.

SOCRATES All right, then, what about equipment? Which kind is it more fitting for a person to find himself with? The kind with which he performs poorly of his own free will or against his will?

HIPPIAS Of his own free will.

SOCRATES Isn't that the case with a bow and a lyre and wind instruments and everything else there is?

HIPPIAS It's the truth you're stating.

SOCRATES Well then, which is superior when it comes to a horse's character? Does someone want to own a horse that he'll be riding poorly at will? Or unwillingly?

HIPPIAS At will.

SOCRATES Then this horse is superior?

HIPPIAS Yes.

SOCRATES Then with a horse who has a superior character, any worthless acts performed by that character would be willing on the rider's part, but unwilling if the horse's character is a worthless one?

HIPPIAS That's surely the case.

SOCRATES And doesn't that hold for a dog and every other kind of animal?

HIPPIAS Yes.

SOCRATES And now: If a human being is an archer, is it more excellent for him to have a character such that he willingly fails to hit the target, or unwillingly?

HIPPIAS Willingly.

SOCRATES Such a character is superior for archery?

HIPPIAS Yes.

SOCRATES So a character unwillingly missing the target is more worthless than one that misses willingly?

HIPPIAS That's the case in archery, anyway.

SOCRATES What about medicine? Isn't the character that willingly performs poorly in caring for bodies more skilled in medicine?

HIPPIAS Yes.

SOCRATES Then that character is superior in this field?

HIPPIAS Yes, it's superior.

SOCRATES All right, then. As to the character more skilled at the harp and at wind instruments and at everything else throughout all the field of knowledge, isn't the superior one the one that willingly performs poorly and disgracefully, and goes absolutely wrong, whereas the more worthless character does so unwillingly?

HIPPIAS It appears so.

SOCRATES But surely, I suppose, you would choose the sorts of character, in slaves you owned, that would go wrong and make mischief willingly rather than unwillingly, as these sorts of character are superior in this respect.

HIPPIAS Yes.

SOCRATES All right, then. Wouldn't you and I ourselves want to have a character that's the most fitting?

HIPPIAS Yes.

SOCRATES Would a character, then, be more fitting if it makes mischief and goes the absolute wrong way willingly, or if it does so unwillingly?

HIPPIAS It would be terrible if those who commit crimes willingly are to be "more fitting" than those who do so unwillingly.

SOCRATES But they do appear so, on the basis of what's been said.

HIPPIAS They certainly don't appear so to me.

SOCRATES But I thought, Hippias, that it appeared so to

you too. But answer once more. Is lawfulness an ability of some sort or a field of knowledge, or both? Or is it not necessary for lawfulness to be one of these things?

HIPPIAS No, it's necessary.

SOCRATES So if lawfulness is an ability of the character, the more able character is more lawful? In fact, such a character has appeared to us to be more fitting, my most excellent friend.

HIPPIAS It has, in fact.

SOCRATES What if lawfulness is a field of knowledge? Is not the more intelligent character more lawful, and the more inept character more criminal?

HIPPIAS Yes, they are.

SOCRATES What if lawfulness is both? Is not a character that has both of these things, knowledge and ability, more lawful? This is how it has to work, isn't it?

HIPPIAS It appears so.

SOCRATES Didn't the more able and intelligent character appear superior, and more able to do either fine things or disgraceful things, in every kind of work it performs?

HIPPIAS Yes.

SOCRATES Then whenever it performs disgracefully, it performs willfully, through ability and skill. And these appear to be part of lawfulness, whether it's both of them or just one.

HIPPIAS Apparently.

SOCRATES So, now, to commit a crime is to do something poorly, and not to commit one is a fine thing.

HIPPIAS Yes.

SOCRATES So won't the more able and excellent character, whenever it commits a crime, willfully commit that crime, while the worthless character does so against its will?

HIPPIAS It appears so.

SOCRATES So isn't the excellent man the one who has an excellent character, while his opposite has a poor character?

HIPPIAS Yes.

SOCRATES Then it's the mark of an excellent man to commit crimes willfully, while his opposite does so against his will, if indeed the excellent man has an excellent character.

HIPPIAS Well, he does have an excellent character, at any rate.

SOCRATES Then the person who goes wrong and does disgraceful and criminal things, if he does exist, can't be anyone other than the excellent person.

HIPPIAS It's impossible for me to agree with you on that point, Socrates.

SOCRATES I don't even agree with myself, Hippias. But as things are, it necessarily appears that way to us, based on the argument. However, as I was saying before, I'm lost, wandering back and forth on these issues, and I can never settle on a single opinion about them. But it's not at all amazing that I'm lost, or that the man on the street is. However, if you, the intelligent people, are lost too, then at this stage we find ourselves in a pretty terrible situation: not even when we come to you can we find our way again.

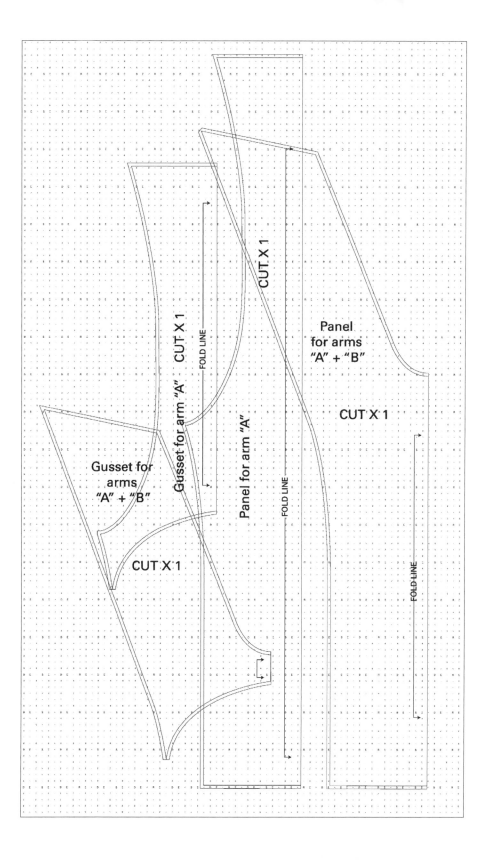

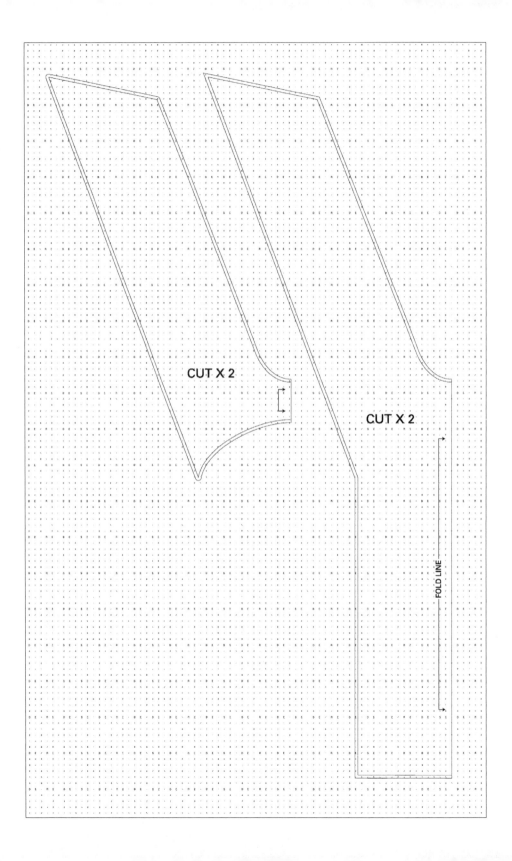

CUT X 2

CUT X 2

FOLD LINE

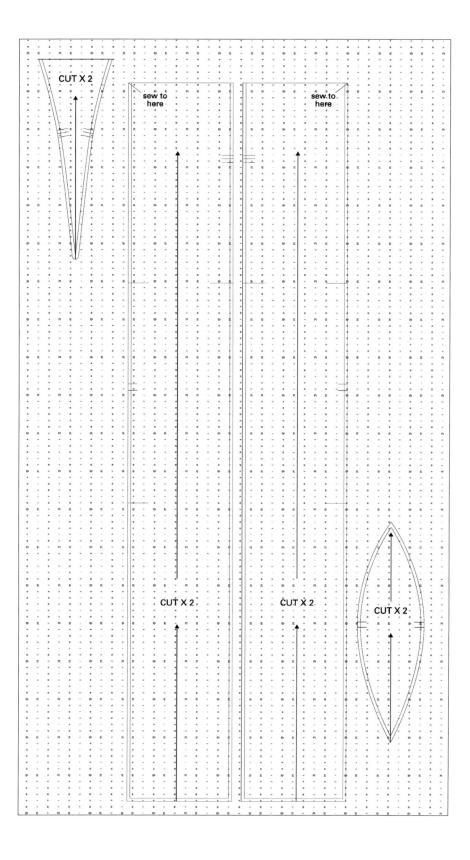

CUT X 2

sew to here

sew to here

CUT X 2

CUT X 2

CUT X 2

SOCRATES 420

by Richard Fletcher

whatever the content in whatever the form, art is only ever interested in appearing as one thing: freedom

—PAUL CHAN[1]

Paul Chan's exploration of art's freedom underpins all of his work and informs his multiple roles as artist and activist, writer and publisher. The exhibition at the DESTE Slaughterhouse on Hydra[2] and the book *Hippias Minor or the Art of Cunning* are no exception. Through a deep engagement with Socrates's perplexing debate with the sophist Hippias on the ethics of willful wrongdoing, Chan declares his dedication to the emancipatory power of art in the hypothesis that art's freedom is based on the key concept of cunning.

1. Paul Chan, *Selected Writings 2000–2014* (New York: Badlands Unlimited; Basel: Schaulager, Laurenz Foundation, 2014), 73.
2. *Hippias Minor*. DESTE Projectspace Slaughterhouse, Hydra, Greece. 6/15–9/30/15.

During 2014 Chan delivered a two-part lecture called "Odysseus as Artist"[3] in various academic contexts in Europe and the United States. At the same time, the *Selected Works* exhibition at the Schaulager in Basel[4] included a radical book project called *New New Testament*,[5] which comprised part of a striking installation as two reading posts facing the earlier work *Volumes*.[6] By incorporating *New New Testament* within the exhibition space, Chan hints at how his publications break free of the museum bookshop and directly resonate with other works in the galleries (e.g., the installations *Arguments* and *Nonprojections*[7] and the two-channel video *Teh Cat n Teh Owl*[8]).

3. Paul Chan, "Odysseus as Artist, Parts I and II." Unpublished lectures. All subsequent quotations are from the versions delivered at the University of Basel, Switzerland, in February and April 2014.

4. *Selected Works*. Schaulager, Basel, Switzerland. 4/12–10/19/14.

5. Paul Chan, *New New Testament* (New York: Badlands Unlimited; Basel: Schaulager, Laurenz Foundation, 2014).

6. Paul Chan, *Volumes*, 2012 (an installation consisting of 1005 painted book covers). Oil on fabric, paper, and synthetic leather, dimensions variable.

7. Since 2013 Chan has created installation works that make use of different configurations of electric cords and sockets plugged into various objects, such as shoes, cardboard boxes, and, in the case of the *Nonprojections*, projectors (seemingly not projecting anything). In the Schaulager exhibition, the *Arguments* were installed as either self-contained networks or the connective tissue between series of Chan's works, from the lower level to the museum's roof. The titles of the individual manifestations of these two series of works are often directly connected to *New New Testament*. For more information on these series, see Paul Chan, *Selected Works* (Basel: Laurenz Foundation, 2014), 337–76.

8. Paul Chan, *Teh Cat n Teh Owl*, 2014. Two-channel video (color, silent), 5h 59'.

"Odysseus as Artist" offers the most immediate background for Chan's engagement with Plato's *Hippias Minor*, since a defense of Odysseus's cunning (*polutropia*) in Homer's *Odyssey* is taken up by Plato's Socrates in a challenge to the sophist Hippias's attacks. This connection is also framed by the way in which Chan engages with ancient philosophical thinkers, traditions, and movements in *New New Testament* and related recent works included in the Schaulager exhibition.

In "Odysseus as Artist" Chan analyzes the episode in Homer's *Odyssey* in which Odysseus finally escapes the island of Calypso by means of his cunning. Chan employs Homer's portrayal of Odysseus's escape to develop his own hypothesis about art's freedom grounded in cunning. Confronted with the excesses of the contemporary art world, Chan argues that we need to join Odysseus in using our cunning to escape from "the seduction of material luxuries, notions of what constitutes a good life, and how these notions entrap ways of thinking and doing."[9] Chan here is attacking not merely the escalating financial excesses of the art market but also how the public discourse about art has become grounded in its own luxuriousness.

It is Chan's hypothesis that the way to counter the reality and perception of the luxuriousness of the contemporary art world is to revitalize and renew art's unique capacity for cunning.

9. Chan, "Odysseus as Artist, Part I."

He opts for "cunning" as a translation of the pivotal Greek word *polutropia*—which more literally means "many twists and turns"—because it articulates a two-action process whereby it locates the "aesthetic imperative within reason itself," and then "situates aesthetics in a truly expanded field."[10] Here, Chan's language owes a debt to Adorno's *Aesthetic Theory*, which he acknowledges at the opening of the first part of the lecture with a discussion of Adorno's aphoristic phase "echo reconciles":

> This is how echo reconciles. In turning elements into echoes of themselves within the matrix of its composition, a work loosens the grip social reality holds over those elements and frees them from their fate, or their pre-existing uses and meanings. They lose, in other words, their natural place in the order of things, which enables them to relate and belong in ways neither wholly predictable nor determined. This is what Adorno believes is one of the most emancipatory aspects of art. It is able to create new relationships out of what already exists to remind us what is still possible with what is naturally given.[11]

10. Chan, "Odysseus as Artist, Part II."
11. Chan, "Odysseus as Artist, Part I."

Chan here redirects what Adorno elsewhere calls "the unfolding of the inner law of those artworks through interpretation, commentary, and critique"[12] into an ethical action which the artist must embrace as a way of life. Furthermore, given that Chan's description of how a work of art, "within the matrix of its composition," frees itself from "pre-existing uses and meanings," it is especially significant that he utilizes a classic work such as Homer's *Odyssey*. The same can be claimed for *Hippias Minor or the Art of Cunning*, which makes the next step in Chan's investigation of art's freedom by means of the art of cunning and the cunning of art operative as its inner law.

This hypothesis about art's emancipatory cunning presented in "Odysseus as Artist" is developed and tested through several of Chan's recent artworks by means of an expanded field that mirrors the transition from Homer's *Odyssey* to Plato's *Hippias Minor*. Chan demonstrates his own capacity for cunning in his engagement with the expanded field of the ancient Greek philosophical tradition. For example, in *New New Testament* and the works *Arguments*, *Nonprojections*, and *Teh Cat n Teh Owl*, Chan examines not only the network of Athenian schools and movements (e.g., Plato's Academy, Aristotle's Lyceum, Zeno's Stoa, Epicurus's Garden, and Diogenes's cosmopolitan Cynicism) but also its later

12. Theodor W. Adorno, *Aesthetic Theory* (London: Bloomsbury Academic, 1997), 399.

translation and transmission in antiquity (e.g., through maxims, handbooks, and commentaries in the Roman Empire).[13]

Consider the section of *New New Testament* in which the following text-work accompanies the gutted and painted book cover of a tome called *The Academy*: [14]

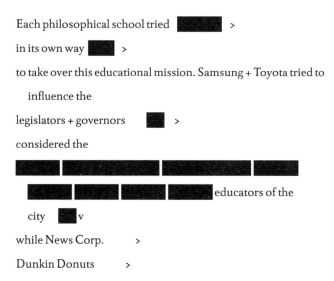

Each philosophical school tried ▓▓▓▓▓ >

in its own way ▓▓▓ >

to take over this educational mission. Samsung + Toyota tried to
  influence the

legislators + governors ▓▓ >

considered the

▓▓▓ ▓▓▓▓▓ ▓▓▓▓▓ ▓▓▓

▓▓▓ ▓▓▓ ▓▓▓ ▓▓▓ educators of the
  city ▓ v

while News Corp. >

Dunkin Donuts >

---

13. For an account of how the transition between Greek and Roman worlds of thought is mapped onto Chan's recent Schaulager exhibition, see Daniel Birnbaum, "Darkness at Noon," in Chan, *Selected Works*.

14. Chan, *New New Testament*, 542 (4.01). All subsequent references to this work will be made not by page but by work number, which can now be searched on badlandsunlimited.com by typing the work number into the search engine at the top of the homepage. You can also use the search engine to find names and concepts as well. Try "Miley Cyrus," "Bob Dylan," "art," "love," "freedom," or "egg."

+ Gristedes tried to convert all the

people ███ > ███

with no distinctions of sex or social condition   >

by means of missionary propaganda.

███ ███

███

As elsewhere in *New New Testament*, Chan transforms accounts of ancient philosophical history into a contemporary critique. From their description, the South Korean multinational conglomerate Samsung and Japanese car manufacturer Toyota appear to replace Plato's Academy and Aristotle's Lyceum; while News Corp. is the new system of Stoicism, Dunkin Donuts the Epicure's delight, and the small Manhattan-based grocery chain Gristedes a capitalist's version of Cynicism.[15]

This network of updated ancient philosophical schools spreads throughout Chan's other works and the Schaulager exhibition as a whole. For example, *The Argument: Athens*[16] seems to represent the topography of the ancient city through a cluster of doors, wiring, sockets, and cardboard boxes. Both *Nonprojections*

15. For more information, see Pierre Hadot, *What Is Ancient Philosophy?*, trans. Michael Chase (Cambridge, MA: Harvard University Press, 2002), 212.
16. Paul Chan, *The Argument: Athens*, 2012–13. Cords, doors, chairs, and cardboard, 83 x 120 x 85 inches.

and the "owl" screen of *Teh Cat n Teh Owl* target the hallowed names of the philosophers themselves (e.g., Socrates becomes "Sock N Tease" or "Cockrateaze"). Furthermore, the "cat" screen of *Teh Cat n Teh Owl* is the sententious sayings of philosophical wisdom reworked; the renowned inscription of the oracle of Delphi, which was the source for Socrates's philosophical mission, becomes "kno thigh seif."

In these works Chan's hypothesis of art's emancipatory cunning is tested by means of his own artistic freedom in remaking the ancient philosophical tradition. Yet at the same time, this is not a simplistic parody or lambasting of the august authority of the classical heritage but a proof of how cunning operates within reason itself—as part of philosophy's inner law. With *Hippias Minor or the Art of Cunning*, as well as extending the reach of the analysis in "Odysseus as Artist," Chan highlights how Plato mobilizes his own cunning art (the dialogue form) to portray Socrates in a way that challenges the established norms that surround him.

Chan is directly intervening in a scholarly debate among classicists who have found the figure of Socrates and his argument in *Hippias Minor* especially enigmatic and confusing. How can Plato portray a coy, devious Socrates who argues that the person who does wrong willingly is a better person than the one who does wrong unwillingly? Readers have either been horrified by the immorality inherent in Socrates's position or have dismissed the whole dialogue as no more than a trifle, nothing to be taken seriously.[17] Obviously there have been valiant scholarly attempts to explain away the enigma, since we classicists are resilient people who love to track back over the well-trodden paths of ancient texts and tell our eminent predecessors where they took a wrong turn.[18] However, none offer the stimulation and significance of Chan's intervention, as I hope to show in the present reading of his work and the dialogue.

In the first section of what follows, I highlight the cunning of Plato's dialogic art, and how that cunning can be read at the level of the inner law of the dialogue—that is, the matrix of its composition in terms of its setting, characterization, and argument. In the second part, I focus on the inner law of the figure of Socrates himself and how the argument that Socrates makes in *Hippias Minor* actually paves the way for the inner law of philosophy in

17. See David Corey, "The Sophist Hippias and the Problem of *Polytropia*," in *Socratic Philosophy and Its Others*, edited by Christopher Dustin and Denise Schaeffer, 91–114 (Lanham, MD: Lexington Books, 2013), III, nn. 9 and 10. Corey relates two formative views of the dialogue: on the one hand, Wilamowitz (1919), "an exquisitely humorous little work with no moral content"; on the other, Apelt (1912), "a kind of apologia for sin" in its "reversal of all moral ideas."

18. Two examples are Charles H. Kahn, "Vlastos's Socrates," Phronesis 37, no. 2 (1992) vs. Gregory Vlastos, "The Hippias Minor – Sophistry or Honest Perplexity?" in Socrates: Ironist and Moral Philosopher, 275–80 (Ithaca: Cornell University Press, 1991) and Corey, "The Sophist Hippias and the Problem of Polytropia," vs. Laurence Lampert, "Socrates' Defense of Polytropic Odysseus: Lying and Wrong-doing in Plato's Lesser Hippias," The Review of Politics 64, no. 2 (2002).

general, as articulated by Plato's Socrates in the *Republic*, with its discussion of aesthetics and ethics.

†

I. SETTING

A country road. A tree. Evening.

—Samuel Beckett, *Waiting for Godot*

Hippias Minor opens with a certain Eudicus addressing Socrates as follows:

> But you, Socrates—how about it? Why aren't you saying anything? Hippias has given such a great presentation, and you won't join in praising anything that's been said— and you won't put him to the test if something doesn't seem fine to you? A special reason for you to speak up is that it's actually just us on our own here, the people most entitled to claim a share in the pursuit of ideas.[19]

19. 363a (47). Sarah Ruden's new translation of *Hippias Minor* uses Bruno Vancamp, *Platon: Hippias maior, Hippias minor: Textkritisch herausgegeben von Bruno Vancamp* (Stuttgart: F. Steiner Verlag, 1996), the recent edition of the Greek text, which revises John Burnet, *Platonis Opera*, Vol. 3 (Oxford: Oxford University Press, 1922).

Unlike Hippias and Socrates, nothing is known about this Eudicus, except what is revealed during the action of the dialogue.[20] Even so, Plato gives him the pivotal role of initiating the dialogue between the sophist Hippias and the philosopher Socrates. In fact, a careful consideration of how Eudicus's opening statement plays out in the first exchanges of the dialogue to come shows how Plato uses this minor character to make a cunning observation about the artistic form of the dialogue, especially as an artistic intervention within the political and cultural contexts of its setting.

Scholars have confirmed that the action of *Hippias Minor* was set during the spring of 420 BCE, when Hippias visited Athens, possibly as part of an embassy from his native city of Elis—at that time an ally of Sparta—during the hiatus in hostilities in the Peloponnesian War known as the Peace of Nicias.[21] *Hippias Major*, set two days prior to *Hippias Minor*, opens with Hippias explaining his absence from Athens, and an earlier visit to Sparta. The success of the Elian embassy to Athens, and the breakdown of relations between Elis and Sparta, may be gleaned from the fact that Hippias was on his way to compete in the Olympic Games,

---

20. We discover that his father, Apemantus, was an authority on Homer. We can also read the valence of his name as euphemistically "well-adjudicating," on which, see F. Zenon Culverhouse, "Plato's 'Hippias Minor': A Translation and Critical Commentary" (PhD diss., Claremont Graduate University, 2010), 18.

21. For a succinct account of this political setting, see Lampert, "Socrates' Defense of Polytropic Odysseus," 232–36.

which the Elians were hosting and from which Sparta had been banned.

While any explicit reference to this context is absent from the opening of *Hippias Minor*, it becomes part of the matrix of composition of Plato's cunning art of dialogue in a way that parallels Chan's own project *Waiting for Godot in New Orleans*.[22] His involvement in the staging of Beckett's *Godot*[23] must be contextualized within its broader political and cultural contexts in the immediate aftermath of Hurricane Katrina. However, in his essay "The Unthinkable Community," Chan frames the Beckett performance within a network of art, pedagogy, and activism by discussing his work in relation to related activities in New Orleans: the classes he taught in local universities as well as his role in the creation of The Front, an artist-run gallery and collective.[24] Concerned with bridging political and aesthetic communities, Chan also contextualizes his own work in terms of a tradition that includes Sade and Bataille. As such, "The Unthinkable Community" not only describes the work but also intervenes in its interpretation via these traditions. Like Chan, Plato makes Eudicus's introduction do similar work for his dialogue.

22. For a detailed account of this 2007 project, including research materials, photographs, drawings, writings, and other documents, see Paul Chan, *Waiting for Godot in New Orleans: A Field Guide* (New York: Creative Time Books, 2010).

23. *Waiting for Godot*, by Samuel Beckett, directed by Christopher McElroen, Lower Ninth Ward and Gently, New Orleans, LA, 11/2–11/10/07.

24. Chan, *Selected Writings*, 90–103.

(i)   The Pursuit of Ideas

As the crowd files out after Hippias's "presentation" (*epideixis*), Eudicus turns to the silent Socrates to ask why he doesn't test the sophist using his signature method of "examination" (*elenchus*), now that they are in the intimate community of "discourses in philosophy" (*tēs en philosophia diatribēs*). Plato's setting neatly juxtaposes three different methodologies for the presentation of ideas, each occupying its own role in the history of ancient philosophy: the sophistic *epideixis*, Socratic *elenchus*, and Platonic *philosophia*. The self-referential gesture by Plato, insinuating his own ongoing innovations in the presentation of philosophical ideas into a conversation set in 420 BCE, is of course a cunning anachronism. Even an attempt to avoid making this anachronism explicit through the translation "pursuit of ideas" would still preempt the Platonic definition of philosophy as "the pursuit of the Ideas" (or Forms) and the knowledge gained from such a pursuit.[25] As an analogy, imagine a documentary film that shows a sequence of experts holding forth on a particular topic, either as individual talking heads or gathered around a dinner table as if at some kind of symposium. Sometimes these experts may by prompted or questioned by an off-camera interviewer, which makes them change their minds or move on to

25. Andrea Wilson Nightingale, *Genres in Dialogue: Plato and the Construct of Philosophy* (Cambridge: Cambridge University Press, 1995), 19 n. 18.

a different topic. Suddenly a voice-over intervenes with a comment about the challenges of making precisely this kind of documentary film. In such a way, Plato's reference to *philosophia* through Eudicus's words acts as a comparable self-referential gesture.

(ii) *Olympic Performances*

Hippias responds to Eudicus's invitation to entertain Socrates's questioning by recalling his previous visits to the Olympic Games, where he would deliver any prepared speech anyone asked for, followed by a question-and-answer session. The Olympic Games were part of the "festival circuit" for intellectuals in general, and the sophists in particular. Moreover, Plato's reference to Hippias's performances at the games may have originated from the fact that he was the author of the first complete list of Olympic victors (*Anagraphe*), which traced back to 776 BCE.[26] There is also a politically sensitive aspect to Hippias's *Anagraphe*. In this work, Hippias claimed that the Spartan lawgiver Lycurgus founded the first Olympics, which gave Sparta a key role in forming the legacy of the games.

Therefore, read within the context of Hippias's political engagement with Sparta in the wider setting of *Hippias Minor*,

---

26. On the Olympics as part of the intellectuals' festival circuit, see Minos Kokolakis, "Intellectual Activity on the Fringes of the Games," in *Proceedings of an International Symposium on the Olympic Games, 5–9 September 1988*, ed. William Coulson and Helmut Kyrieleis (Athens: Deutsches Archäologisches Institut, 1992), 153–58.

Plato's reference to his intellectual activities at the games initiates the markedly Platonic critique of the troubling confusion of political and intellectual activity by the sophists.[27] To again offer an analogy, imagine a documentary film about the Olympics focusing on Adolf Hitler's infamous Berlin games of 1936, which explores the political nature of sport by alternating Leni Riefenstahl's shots of saluting athletes with Nazi soldiers. Suddenly a voice-over intervenes by referencing Eliza Marian Butler's 1935 book, *The Tyranny of Greece over Germany*, and Gottfried Benn's 1934 article on the Doric world, in the same breath.[28] In a similar way, Plato presents the intimate relationship between the sophist's politics and his intellectual pursuits.

(iii)   *Marketplace Debates*

After Hippias's description of his Olympian performances, Socrates claims that he didn't want to intervene during the sophist's presentation because he kept losing track of what Hippias was saying and, on account of the big crowd, didn't want to interrupt the

27. On Plato's leading characterization of the sophists in general, see Håkan Tell, *Plato's Counterfeit Sophists* (Cambridge, MA: Center for Hellenic Studies, Harvard University, 2011). See also Chan, *New New Testament*, 1.0035.
28. Compare with the story of the Polish scholar Tardewski in Ricardo Piglia's 1980 novel, *Respiración artificial*. Tardewski orders the works of Hippias from the British Library while working on a project on Heidegger and the Presocratics; instead, he receives *Mein Kampf*, thanks to the disorder of the library catalogue for entries under HI.

presentation with his queries. The image of the perplexed Socrates in attendance at Hippias's presentation highlights an image of the philosopher elsewhere in Plato's dialogues, such as the general situation of the philosopher on trial in his *Apology* and the digression in his *Theaetetus*.[29] His reaction also points to his own intellectual contexts, which, according to the *Apology*, took place "in the public square, next to the bankers' tables."[30] It is no coincidence that this will be exactly the same place where Plato sets Socrates's overhearing of Hippias's boast of his self-sufficiency on an earlier Olympic sojourn.[31]

If Plato represents both the methods of *epideixis* ("presentation") and *elenchus* ("examination") and their practitioners (Hippias and Socrates) as operating outside the democratic political processes of late-fifth-century Athens, the community he creates in his dialogues, involved in the "pursuit of ideas," represents, in itself, a certain kind of political enthusiasm and freedom. To use my recurring analogy one last time, imagine a documentary film that presents footage of the demonstrations of November 3, 1968, in Athens at the funeral of Georgios Papandreou. Suddenly a voice-over intervenes by commenting on how the crowd moved from chanting the name of the dead hero to celebrating the lofty political

---

29. Plato, *Theaetetus* 172c–177c.
30. Plato, *Apology* 17c.
31. 368b (61).

concepts of "freedom" and "democracy." Similarly, the Platonic dialogue moves from the martyred (Socratic) philosopher's ideas to the transcendent Ideas of (Platonic) philosophy.

II. CHARACTERIZATION

> *[Plato] tosses the Hippiases and Gorgiases with*
> *their grand reputations, as a boy tosses his balls.*
> —Ralph Waldo Emerson, *Plato or the Philosopher*

The political and cultural settings of *Hippias Minor* are both put to work in Plato's description of Hippias's Olympic performances and Socrates's marketplace debates, as well as reframed by the novelty of Eudicus's Platonic call for creating a dialogue as a new community in the "pursuit of ideas." This cunning manipulation of setting depends on the dialogue's characters: Hippias, the boastful sophist; Socrates, the ironic philosopher; Eudicus, the hopeful arbiter of a debate between the two.[32] However, appreciating Plato's cunning art in *Hippias Minor* requires an understanding of how such characterization develops throughout the dialogue. As with its setting, it is important to recognize the dynamic between a historical figure like Hippias and the manipulation of this figure for Plato's literary

---

32. For a general discussion of characterization in *Hippias Minor*, see Ruby Blondell, *The Play of Character in Plato's Dialogues* (Cambridge: Cambridge University Press, 2002).

and philosophical ends. However, what differentiates setting and characterization is the fact that Plato was engaging with Hippias not only as a historical figure but also as a writer and thinker. In creating his new portrait of the sophist, he must negotiate the difference between remembering and forgetting the life and works of the real Hippias.

Simultaneous acts of remembering and forgetting figure as a key dynamic in Chan's 7 ~~Lights~~ series,[33] from the strikethrough as a graphic negation of its title to the *7th ~~Light~~* as an unrealized score. As George Baker has masterfully shown, 7 ~~Lights~~ brims with references to earlier art history and to Chan's previous works.[34] On a more general level, there have been less nuanced attempts to make 7 ~~Lights~~ into a kind of artistic memorial for the terrorist attacks of September 11. Chan responds to both forms of reference and memorialization in his essay "Forget September," a brief but powerful piece that articulates, in the form of debt, an alternative to memory and forgetting.[35] In this essay Chan refers to the "notion that what one owes is potentially more socially valuable and productive than what one can make, or who one is." One

---

33. 7 ~~Lights~~ (2005–7) is a series of projections that make use of different configurations of light and shadow to depict various moving figures and objects, such as telephone poles, dogs, and, in the case of the seventh work in the series, musical notes, represented by torn scraps of black paper. For more information, see Chan, *Selected Works*, 337–76.

34. George Baker, "Paul Chan: The Image from Outside," in *Paul Chan: The 7 ~~Lights~~* (Cologne: Walther Koenig, 2007), 4–18.

alternative that Chan entertains as a way out of such a powerful bind is to embrace the situation of indebtedness, to accept that "the bindingness of what we owe to ourselves and others grounds the making of what appears as the present." An implication of Chan's introduction of the idea of indebted identity into the dichotomy of memory and forgetting is the fundamentally tricky issue of Plato's own debts—to Homer, to Socrates, and, most pertinently, to the sophists. This is why the characterization of Hippias cannot be simple parody. Plato owes Hippias, and the dialogue is his way to record and also annul such a debt.[36]

(iv)   Memoirs of a Sophist

After the opening remarks, Hippias announces that he will give a recap of his original *epideixis* "in detail, even more clearly" than the original for Socrates's benefit. After some initial resistance, Socrates learns that Homer depicted Odysseus as both cunning and deceptive, and Achilles as frank and truthful. Socrates begins, obliging Eudicus's request, by testing Hippias on the subject matter of the earlier presentation (i.e., Homer), but as the argument develops, Socrates seeks to challenge Hippias's premise that the deceptive and the truthful person cannot be one and the same, by

35. Chan, *Selected Writings*, 108–10.
36. Compare Chan, *New New Testament*, 1.0032.

shifting to the sophist's expertise in other fields (e.g., arithmetic, geometry, and astronomy). This transition in Hippias's characterization can be mapped onto what we know of a kind of anthology that Hippias was supposed to have written. A fragment from this so-called *Synagoge* ("Collection") runs as follows:

> Some of these things have probably been said by Orpheus, others by Musaeus briefly in different places, yet others by Hesiod and Homer, others by the other poets, others in prose-writings by Greeks and non-Greeks alike. But I will make this account new and varied by putting together the most important and related sayings from all of them.[37]

The anthology of ancient wisdom repurposed in a new way highlights Hippias's two characterizations in *Hippias Minor* as an expert on Homer and as a polymath. As such, Plato is intimating that Hippias's argument about Homer is necessarily restricted by Homer, and so we need Socrates to break out on a new path. To paraphrase Odysseus Elytis's poem "Beautiful and Strange Homeland," Hippias calls for revolution and gives himself tyrants.

---

37. Quoted in Tell, *Plato's Counterfeit Sophists*, 4.

(v)   The Right to Forget and Be Forgotten

Do the polymath Hippias's other abilities offer a viable alternative to his suffocating debt to Homer? One answer lies in Socrates's joke about forgetting Hippias's famous art of memory. After recalling Hippias's boast of his visit to Olympia, wearing only clothes he made himself and displaying his unique range of intellectual and literary skills, Socrates invokes Hippias's memory:

> Oh, but it looks as if I forgot your system for memoriza-
> tion, in which you think yourself most illustrious. And I
> think I've forgotten all manner of other things.[38]

Closely following this reference to Hippias's famous memory, Socrates urges the sophist to defend his position. When Hippias cannot respond, Socrates has to remind him of the argument so far. As we proceed, Socrates demonstrates his memory of Homer to support his argument, and Hippias asks, "Where's that?"[39] The shift in Hippias's characterization, from master of memory to someone who is not only forgetful of the current discussion but the poetry of Homer as well, is a clear example of Plato's own art of cunning characterization. He demonstrates Hippias's ability

38. 368d (62).
39. 371b (67).

to forget (when he wants to), thus "playing the part of Odysseus" in his cunning.[40]

What Plato dramatizes through his deconstruction of the character of Hippias is the basic weakness, not of his abilities, but of his claims to those abilities as a sophist. The final joke about memory is made by the existence of the dialogue itself: the sophist's indebted identity is reliant on the record of an event that may never have taken place, with a version of Hippias that may never have lived. Just as the assassination of the doctor, politician, and athlete Grigoris Lambrakis in 1963 inadvertently made him a legend—living on in his symbolic letter "Z," an icon in future political demonstrations, memorialized in Vassilis Vassilikos's novel, and immortalized in Costa-Gavras's film—so too does Hippias live on in Plato's dialogue.

III. ARGUMENT

... a tedious argument / Of insidious intent
—T. S. Eliot, "The Love Song of J. Alfred Prufrock"

In both his setting and characterization of *Hippias Minor* we have witnessed Plato's cunning art in alternating between methodologies (i.e., *epideixis* and *elenchus*) and abilities (i.e., memory and

40. 370e (66).

forgetting) as well as the creation of new models of thinking (e.g., the pursuit of ideas, the indebtedness of identity) at the heart of the Platonic dialogue. However, what remains to be unraveled is the knotty issue of Socrates's argument itself. Can we point to Plato's cunning art of dialogue as the reason why he makes his Socrates argue so badly for the moral supremacy of the willful wrongdoer?

It would be a mistake to completely separate "literary" forms of setting and characterization from the "philosophical" content of the argument. Nonetheless, it is still difficult to see how Plato's cunning literary devices can be used as a means of escaping the most enigmatic part of the dialogue, which has been attacked since Aristotle's testimony.[41] Instead, with Chan's reading of Adorno, what must be focused on is the cunning at work within reason itself; that is, within the argument of *Hippias Minor*.

One of Chan's works that articulates this tension within philosophical argument is *Sade for Sade's Sake*,[42] especially in its application to Plato's *Phaedrus* in the book *Phaedrus Pron*.[43] Chan took Plato's erotic dialogue and transposed it using several of his alternumeric fonts, which replaced individual letters and numbers

---

41. Aristotle, *Metaphysics* 1025a.

42. Paul Chan, *Sade for Sade's Sake*, 2009. Three-channel digital video projection (color, silent), 5h 45'. For more information on this project, see Paul Chan, *The Essential and Incomplete Sade for Sade's Sake* (New York: Badlands Unlimited, 2010).

43. Paul Chan, *Phaedrus Pron* (New York: Badlands Unlimited, 2010).

(known as alphanumerics) with textual and graphic fragments inspired by Sade's work. In this way Chan brought Plato's lofty discussion of love and rhetoric down to its primal level—the moans and groans of sexual desire. At the same time as manipulating a philosophical argument, Chan made a direct connection between the erotic and the aesthetic, the body and its gracefulness, that will come to resonate in *Hippias Minor* as well.

(vi)   *False Premises and Fallacious Inferences*

Socrates's argument in *Hippias Minor* has been described as being based on two false premises and supported by two fallacious inferences, and as reaching a paradoxical conclusion.[44] Socrates defines the false man as the man who is capable of speaking falsely and claims the true and false man are one and the same. From these premises he infers that there is an equivocation of the good and that the voluntary wrongdoer is (morally) superior to the involuntary wrongdoer. To offer the example of first inference, it is fallacious on several counts. On the one hand, the fact that a person is "good" at something (e.g., running) does not necessarily make them "good" in general, because the proposition "A is good at X-ing" does not evaluate character (or even performance), but capacity alone. On

44. John Beversluis, *Cross-Examining Socrates: A Defense of the Interlocutors in Plato's Early Dialogues* (Cambridge: Cambridge University Press, 2000), 107–9.

the other hand, the implication that someone who voluntarily fails to do what they are capable of doing, who voluntarily misuses his *technē* ("skill," "craft"), overlooks the important distinction between the misuse and nonuse of a *technē*. For example, the doctor who misuses his *technē* to poison a patient is markedly different from the wrestler who wrestles poorly to lose his bout. The wrestler does not misuse his *technē*; rather, he does not use it at all.

The fallacy of the equivocation of the term "good" can however be explained away if one makes a distinction between denoting a person's moral disposition or character and describing a morally neutral capacity or ability. The former avoids the fallacy, but in doing so requires that Hippias make an argument in response to Socrates that he does not make, one that is conveniently bound up with what the sophists thought rhetoric was. In short, boiling the dialogue down to the bones of its arguments does not prevent the main uncertainty from arising. Why is Plato making his Socrates argue in this way? And why portray the protests of Hippias, the enemy sophist, as legitimate? And amid the sound and the fury of Plato's cunning art of dialogue, is there even a need for a single answer?

(vii)   *Outdueling the Sophist with Sophistry*

If we save Socrates from dealing in false premises and fallacious inferences, do we need to make him into a sophist—or have him outduel the sophist with sophistry? The opposite extreme is to emphasize Socrates's "honest perplexity," possibly of the self-induced variety.[45] This latter reading has been challenged in an interesting way, as it is "blind . . . to the malicious humor and flagrant bluffing of *Hippias Minor*."[46] Yet the former idea, of Socrates the sophist, is supported by a variation of the argument used to defeat the fallacy of equivocation. The distinction between ability and character is part of the general question of rhetoric and sophistry. Like any *technē*, it can be misused, and the error lies in the misuser (their character) and not the *technē* itself. But for Plato's Hippias, who targets Odysseus's cunning as an ability that makes him (morally) dubious, can rhetoric, which may be deemed neutral in itself, impart knowledge of the highest good, as claimed by Plato's Gorgias and Protagoras, or the opposite?[47] With Hippias's rejection of the neutrality of capacity—in speaking or in any other ability—opens up a division within the sophistic ranks, which could allow for Socrates's support. Even the caricature of the sophist as fencing to win, regardless of truth, does not mean that Plato's Socrates cannot exploit every means to win, with every consent, a surrender. So, when both logic and logomachy fail to make sense of the argument of *Hippias Minor*, where can we turn?

45. Vlastos, "The *Hippias Minor* – Sophistry or Honest Perplexity?," 275–79.
46. Kahn, "Vlastos's Socrates," 253.
47. *Gorgias* 454b–c; *Protagoras* 319a–b.

(viii)   The Inner Law

If Socrates's argument is not fallacious and if he is not merely trying to outduel the sophist with sophistry, then what is going on? Does the "terrible" (*deinos*) conclusion, in Hippias's phrasing, mean that the only way is to side with Hippias?[48] Or can Plato's Socrates be redeemed?

At the end of the first round of arguments, when Hippias resists Socrates's conclusion—that those who deceive willingly are more fitting persons than those who do so unwillingly—he does so with the following recourse to the law:

> And the laws are in fact much harsher toward those who wilfully perform evil acts and practice deception than toward the unwilling.[49]

This could just be Hippias keeping up appearances, wanting to *be seen* to be doing what is right by alluding to traditional values—that is, the law. Even so, what happens if Hippias's reference to the laws is applied to Socrates, and we look at his argument in the same way that Adorno's conception of the "inner law" has been applied to Plato's cunning art of dialogue?

48. 376c (83).
49. 372a (68).

Socrates's response to the invocation of the laws by Hippias is to look to an inner law by describing his *psuchē* ("soul," "character") as being "inept" and in need of being "put in a better state."[50] The idea of the inner law or orderliness of one's character is central to the discussion of the tyrant in Plato's *Republic* as a figure governed by the appetitive part of the soul, who thus behaves in a tyrannical way. Yet the discussion in *Hippias Minor* most closely corresponds to Socrates's answer to Callicles in Plato's *Gorgias*:

> For I, my good sir, would rather have my lyre or my chorus out of tune or discordant, or have many human beings disagree with me and contradict me, than that I, being one, should be in discord and contradict myself.[51]

In what follows, on reaching this crucial point in the dialogue, it is the question of the harmony of Socrates's soul and his focus on this inner law that should be the main focus of the argument. Yet this is not what happens. Instead, the only glimmer of this alternative argument is found in a single word, a word that Plato's Socrates uses to describe the body, but which, in other dialogues, expands quickly to describe character, morality, and the Good. It is at this startling moment in *Hippias Minor* that previous organizing principles must

50. 372e–373a (70).
51. *Gorgias* 482b–c.

be abandoned, from strange analogies of documentary films to random comments about modern Greek history and poetry. There will be no musings on the order of the cosmos, the realm of myth, or the snares of desire, nor the violence of tragedy. Only the triumph of philosophy remains, and it takes a very intriguing path, straight to the heart of Chan's hypothesis of art's cunning.

† †

IV. SOCK N TEASE

i h8 hippocrates[52]

The literary setting, characterization, and philosophical argument of *Hippias Minor* all cohere at this point: Socrates's inner law. But what exactly is it? And why has it been overlooked in earlier readings of the dialogue? The answer is that there is a key moment in the argument, during the second half of the dialogue, which Hippias and the majority of Plato's readers have missed, but which settles Socrates in a way that can allow him to continue unperturbed by his original argument's conclusions. Furthermore, it is the connection between Socrates's inner law, in particular, and philosophy's inner law, in general, that Plato pinpoints at this overlooked moment.

52. Chan, *Teh Cat n Teh Owl*.

Chan's new works, the *Nonprojections*, with their ghostly evocation of image production without the image, have been received as a radical departure from his previous practice. Yet the defacement of ancient philosophers' names in the titles of these works unites these installations with the comparable process in the "owl" channel of *Teh Cat n teh Owl*. "Play Doh" becomes "Playdoz"; "Die All Jennie," "Diogenius"; "Sock N Tease," naturally, "Cockrateaze." This work, Chan's most explicit homage to Chris Marker to date, projects further abuse on the hallowed names of the *Nonprojections* in a way that questions both the signifier and the signified. Philosophy as the owl's legacy has become manipulated in a way that compares with the specific case of Chan's own trajectory as an artist. In other words, what ties the *Nonprojections* and *Teh Cat n teh Owl* together is precisely the expanded field of art's cunning.

After Socrates's interlude on his ineptitude, Plato returns to the argument. But this time the memory of Hippias's original presentation fades away and there will be no more direct grappling with Homer, or his presentation of Achilles or Odysseus, in the remainder of the dialogue. As Socrates's argument continues, he will mirror the movement from Hippias's invocation of the law to his inner law in leaving behind the expansive list of Hippias's abilities (e.g., arithmetic, calculation, geometry, astronomy) for subjects that eventually cohere *within* Hippias himself—his character or soul. It is no surprise that Plato makes this new order argument revisit the scene of the earlier account of Hippias's abilities: the Olympic Games. While, before, Socrates expressed amazement at Hippias's confidence in his ability to compete with his thinking compared to the athlete's ability to compete with his body, at this stage in the dialogue, the tables have turned. Now Socrates will make the body his focus for his inner law at the culmination of a series of athletic examples:

> SOCRATES   But what about gracefulness, Hippias? Is it not characteristic of the more fitting body to willingly assume disgraceful and poor positions, while the poorer body does this unwillingly? Or what do you think?

> HIPPIAS   That's right.

> SOCRATES   Then gracelessness that's willing is meritorious where physical condition is concerned, while gracelessness that's unwilling is a sign of poor physical condition.

> HIPPIAS   That's clear.[53]

When Plato uses the term "gracefulness" (*euschēmosunē*), together with the passing reference to the "excellence" (*aretē*) of the

---

53. 374b–c (74–75).

body—which, elsewhere in Plato, is considered health—it is surprising that only the latter has been highlighted by commentators
as a hint (but only a hint) of the moral valence of the discussion.
For example, Zenon Culverhouse notes: "Socrates may make this
move to hint at the possibility that these claims may be correctly
applied to moral cases, but he only does so in passing."[54] However,
it is the word and concept of *euschēmosunē* that are key here,
because it is the direct effect of harmony—the inner law—that
Socrates desires in himself and Plato for philosophy in his dialogues, as can be better understood through a consideration of its
use in Plato's *Republic*.

Plato's *Republic* is the philosopher's major statement regarding
art and its role in society. It also is the most extended treatment of
the Platonic theory of the tripartite and immortal soul. In Book 3,
Plato makes the connection between the character or soul and
mimetic artistic production through the concept of "gracefulness"
(*euschēmosunē*), amid the discussion of the role of the arts in the
education of the guardians:

> SOCRATES   Fine speech, then, and well-tempered harmony
> and gracefulness (*euschēmosunē*) and good rhythm go together
> with good-heartedness (*euetheia*)—I don't mean idiocy (*anoia*)

---

54. Culverhouse, "Plato's 'Hippias Minor'," 307.

which we mockingly call "euetheia,"[55] rather, as is truly good and fitting, I make thought the *ethos* in *euetheia*.

GLAUCON Absolutely.

SOCRATES Well then, are these things not to be pursued by young men if they are going to do the work that is truly theirs?

GLAUCON Yes, they must indeed.

SOCRATES And painting is full of these things, as are such crafts: weaving and embroidery and architecture and the manufacture of all tools, and even the nature of bodies and that of all creatures, for in all of these there is gracefulness (*euschēmosunē*) or the lack of it. And lack of grace and rhythm and harmony are akin to malformed reason and bad character, while their opposites are akin to imitations of temperate and good character.[56]

---

55. Here we find Plato's art of cunning in a nutshell. He corrects the common meaning of *euetheia* as "simplemindedness" by making it mean "good-heartedness" through the philosophically uplifting connection with *ethos* ("character"). Note that Plato makes Hippias use the term *euetheia* to describe Achilles; see 371e (68).
56. *Republic* 400d–401a.

In the passage that follows, using the example of educating children, Socrates claims that good habits can be instilled in their "souls" by immersing them in forms of beauty, such as the arts (especially music), because:

> SOCRATES   Rhythm and harmony permeate the inner-most
> element of the soul and take an incredibly powerful grip on
> it, bringing and bestowing gracefulness (*euschēmosunē*) if the
> education is right, and bestowing the reverse if it is not.[57]

To return to *Hippias Minor* with these passages in mind, it becomes clear that the first part of the dialogue is less focused on the goodness or badness of telling the truth or lying, but instead highlights the ability or capacity to do either or both of these things. In the second half of the dialogue, however, there is a clear emphasis on the opposition between the goodness or badness of the action done. Yet within this dichotomy that toggles between ideas of capacity and morality, and which has been the main point of contention in Plato's readers, there is also an aesthetic duality—of gracefulness and gracelessness—that has been almost completely overlooked. Perhaps the reason for this is that the aesthetic language used in Plato's Republic to describe painting, architecture, and poetry,

57. *Republic* 401d–e.

is, in *Hippias Minor*, used only in reference to the body.[58] Yet this understandable oversight has major implications. It means that Socrates remains trapped within his perplexing and sophistic argument in *Hippias Minor* and cannot be freed to deploy the broader ambitions of Platonic philosophy.

V. BOB DYLAN

> *The texts began to shimmer and unravel, becoming*
> *like what someone who did not know how words were*
> *meant to work would compose: by feel and by necessity.*
> —Paul Chan[59]

Once the enigma of the argument of *Hippias Minor* has been discovered in the dynamic between Socrates's inner law and bodily gracefulness, we can see Chan's hypothesis of art's emancipatory cunning at work. Furthermore, by catching sight of the glimmer of Platonic debate about the aesthetic quality of gracefulness in the path not taken in Socrates's argument, we arrive at a liberating understanding of how the dialogue works as a whole. There is no need to separate aspects of "literary" form (i.e., setting and characterization)

---

58. Compare Agathon's speech in Plato's *Symposium*, in which he describes a war between gracefulness and love (196a).
59. Chan, *New New Testament*, 14.

from those of philosophical content (i.e., the argument), as there is an absolute conflation of aesthetics and ethics at play.

What happens during the space of one word in *Hippias Minor* can be read in every page of *New New Testament*. Its employment of texts that "shimmer and unravel" to accompany the book-canvases of *Volumes* both hides and reveals the rich tapestry of philosophical history and argument that glows from beneath. As such, this work is not merely a rewriting of ancient philosophy for a contemporary audience enamored by the depth and dazzle of Bob Dylan and Miley Cyrus in place of Socrates and Hippias, but a completely new investigation into the philosophy of nature and art.[60] To read *New New Testament* is to simultaneously grasp Chan's unique negotiation of the philosophies of nature, the history of painting, and popular culture.

In fact, these questions of life and art, nature and artifice, are those that Plato's dialogues attempt to break down. Later Platonists knew this more than most. For example, Apuleius of Madauros, in his potted biography of Plato that prefaced his dry handbook *On Plato and His Doctrine*, described how Plato gave birth to philosophy, as if it was his own child, but also crafted it out of all previous thought, like a work of art.[61] Apuleius proceeds

---

60. See Chan, *New New Testament*, 1.00002 and 1.0035, with Hadot, *Ancient Philosophy*, 21 and 26.

61. See my *Apuleius' Platonism: The Impersonation of Philosophy* (Cambridge: Cambridge University Press, 2014), 20–22.

to describe how Plato transformed philosophy through the process of filing it down with "reason" (*ratio*) and dressing it up in "speech" (*oratio*).[62] While Proclus, in his commentary on Plato's *Timaeus*, quotes Longinus on the grace of Plato's style:

> At this point Longinus says that Plato employed a decorative style, on account of the bold similes and graceful vocabulary that adorns the diction, making a point against certain Platonists who claim that the style of this passage is something spontaneous, and not something contrived by the philosopher.[63]

A little later, he quotes Origines, who makes the direct connection between the handiwork of the demiurge and Plato's writing:

> Origines agreed that Plato is taking care over the grace of his writing, not however because he is aiming at pleasure, but in the course of using this comparison for the presentation of what he felt . . . the grace of language mirrors the grace that has been instilled into heavenly things by the demiurge.[64]

62. On *ratio et oratio* as the central theme of Apuleius's Platonism, see ibid.
63. Proclus, *Commentary on Plato's* Timaeus, I. 59.
64. Ibid., I. 60.

These interpretations offer a way forward for evaluating *Hippias Minor*, not only as a singular work of literature, but also as part of Plato's network of dialogues.

The prevalent story is of Plato's *Hippias Minor* ending in tragedy, with Socrates out of sorts with himself, in disagreement with the argument he himself has generated and defended, wandering back and forth over the issues at stake, with Hippias's stubborn refusal the only glimmer of hope. But now, thanks to Chan's hypothesis of art's emancipatory cunning, Plato's *Hippias Minor* can end in triumph, with Platonic philosophy freeing Socrates from the argument, from Hippias, from sophists, from Athens. This freedom shimmers with possibility as to how the inner self, the graceful body, and the work of art all cohere in philosophy's inner law.[65]

65. In other words, the liberating fusion of philosophy and art, idea and form, as enacted in the transformation of Greek *logos* ("reason," "speech") into Latin *ratio et oratio* ("reason and speech").

FURTHER READING

This list is designed to provide general introductory reading on the history of Plato's dialogues and *Hippias Minor* in particular.

Balaudé, Jean-François. "Que veut montrer Socrate dans l'*Hippias Mineur?*" In *Lezioni Socratiche*, edited by G. Giannantoni and M. Narcy, 259–77. Naples: Bibliopolis, 1997.

Beversluis, John. "Hippias." In *Cross-Examining Socrates: A defense of the interlocutors in Plato's early dialogues*, 94–110. Cambridge: Cambridge University Press, 2000.

Blondell, Ruby. "The elenctic Sokrates at work: Hippias Minor." In *The Play of Character in Plato's Dialogues*, 113–64. Cambridge: Cambridge University Press, 2002.

Corey, David. "The Sophist Hippias and the Problem of *Polytropia*." In *Socratic Philosophy and Its Others*, edited by Christopher Dustin and Denise Schaeffer, 91–114. Lanham, MD: Lexington Books, 2013.

Culverhouse, F. Zenon. "Plato's 'Hippias Minor': A Translation and Critical Commentary." PhD diss., Claremont Graduate University, 2010.

Kahn, Charles. "Plato as a minor Socratic: *Ion* and *Hippias Minor*." In *Plato and the Socratic Dialogue: The Philosophical Use of a Literary Form*, 101–124. Cambridge: Cambridge University Press, 1996.

Lampert, Laurence. "Socrates' Defense of Polytropic Odysseus: Lying and Wrong-doing in Plato's Lesser *Hippias*." *The Review of Politics* 64, no. 2 (2002): 231–60.

Lévystone, David. "La figure d'Ulysse chez les Socratiques: Socrate *polutropos*." *Phronesis* 50, no. 3 (2005): 181–214.

Mulhern, J. J. "*Tropos* and *Polytropia* in Plato's *Hippias Minor*." *Phoenix* 22 (1968): 283–88.

Pinjuh, Jan-Markus. Platons *"Hippias Minor": Übersetzung und Kommentar von Jan-Markus Pinjuh*. Tübingen: Narr Francke Attempto Verlag, 2014.

Rabaté, Jean-Michel. "White Lies: Plato, Nietzsche, and Hollywood." In *The Ethics of the Lie*, translated by Suzanne Verderber, 111–52. New York: Other Press, 2008.

Vancamp, Bruno. *Platon: Hippias maior, Hippias minor: Textkritisch herausgegeben von Bruno Vancamp*. Stuttgart: F. Steiner Verlag, 1996.

Vlastos, Gregory. "*The Hippias Minor*—Sophistry or Honest Perplexity?" In *Socrates: Ironist and Moral Philosopher*, 275–80. Ithaca: Cornell University Press, 1991.

Weiss, Roslyn. "The *Hippias Minor*: 'If There Be Such a Man'." In *The Socratic Paradox and Its Enemies*, 120–47. Chicago: The University of Chicago Press, 2006.

ABOUT THE CONTRIBUTORS

Sarah Ruden has a doctorate in classics from Harvard and an MA from Johns Hopkins University. She is a poet and freelance writer specializing in the translation of Latin, Greek, and Hebrew literature and has received a Guggenheim Fellowship for this work. Her most recent book is a translation of Apuleius's *The Golden Ass*; a book on the Bible's original texts, and a new translation of St. Augustine's *Confessions*, are forthcoming. She spent around a decade in post-apartheid South Africa and in her journalism takes a special interest in religion and the problems of the developing world. She is currently a visiting scholar at Brown University.

Richard Fletcher is an associate professor in the Department of Classics at Ohio State University. He specializes in the transmission and translation of ancient Greek philosophy into Roman culture and Latin literature, as well as the dynamic between classics and contemporary art. His book *Apuleius' Platonism: The Impersonation of Philosophy* was published by Cambridge University Press in 2014. He is currently editing *The Oxford Handbook of Roman Philosophy* (with Will Shearin).

Paul Chan is an artist based in New York.